Paul Daniels' Magic Book

Paul Daniels often dislikes being called a magician, conjurer or, indeed, a magic man – even though he is all three and more. He prefers to be called a 'Funjurer', one who not only 'conjures' up magical mysteries left, right and centre, but 'conjures' up his own style of comedy and wit at the same time.

Paul likes the way things are happening to him – not a lot; but he likes it! In a matter of four years Paul has become the number one magician (funjurer) in Britain and is gradually becoming internationally known as a 'sparkling entertainer' with a glowing personality.

The wide variety of magic which he presents so expertly on his own television programmes has achieved him much fame and distinction.

Here, in his first book of magic, Paul Daniels discloses some of his secrets together with solid professional advice for the beginner, on how to perform magic tricks properly and entertainingly.

Whilst he is known as a 'funny man', Paul takes his profession very seriously. He simply hates seeing tricks and illusions performed badly – even by some of the top magicians!

A clever 'close-up' conjurer, a most accomplished cabaret and television performer, and a witty television panellist, Paul Daniels has so much to offer.

He now offers readers some of the most entertaining tricks and mysteries ever seen. Many have been specially devised for his book and Paul's own touch of originality shines through.

Treat his magic and secrets with loving care – they will serve you well. Whenever you wish to entertain small groups at home, larger groups at school, or even larger crowds at concerts and local fêtes, his magic will always make their eyes pop out!

But please remember Paul's 'Password' – *Keep the secrets secret, or they won't be secret any more!*

Paul Daniels

Paul Daniels' **Magic** Book

Scholastic Publications Ltd
in association with Pan Books

ACKNOWLEDGEMENT

In writing this, my very first book of magic, I would like to thank my magical pal IAN ADAIR, clever magical inventor and writer, for his wonderful assistance in preparing some of the material described. He's a super fellow – and as a magical adviser, one could not look for anyone better. How he's managed to find time to write his already published 73 books on magic must surely be a trick on its own.

But then, we magic men are always doing the near impossible!

First published 1980 by Pan Books Ltd,
Cavaye Place, London SW10 9PG
Text © Paul Daniels 1980
Illustrations © Roger Walker 1980
Scholastic Publications edition first published 1980
ISBN 0 330 26185 1
Printed in Great Britain by
Richard Clay (The Chaucer Press) Ltd, Bungay, Suffolk

Contents

Introduction —
Welcome to my Book of Magic

Shake hands! Like me, you're interested in magic. That's a good start.

Boys – would you like to know the secret of how to change your little sister into a chocolate frog?

Girls – would you like to learn how to turn your big brother into a live kicking rabbit? You would? – well, you won't find the answers to these problems in *my* book. Nor will you, for example, be able to make a magic wand that, at a single wave, makes Mum and Dad disappear anytime you wish!

My book of magic is simply crammed with goodies – those secrets – tricks, stunts and teasers – which can be made from all sorts of things lying around the house.

I hope you will like my book of magic – not a lot – but that you'll like it!

It's easy to make the tricks I describe and easy to perform them, so that soon you'll be able to do them better than I (that's not so difficult ... eh!).

Magic or conjuring, as it is known (I like to call it 'funjuring'), is made up of many distinctive branches.

There's *'Close-up Magic'* – that's magic done close-up! Lots of professional magicians present such tricks at the table, at home, close-up and surrounded. When I am on the telly (and that's a most uncomfortable position to be in!) I like performing close-up magic, trying to fool millions (well ... I've never really counted them all) using things like matchsticks, coins, paperclips and string.

Card Magic is another branch of the art. I would be lost without a pack of cards – 52 cardboard assistants and one *joker* – no guessing who that is? (What! – how dare you – get stood over there in the corner you little demons – me a joker ... unthinkable!)

There's *Stage and Big Magic* too! Here is the type of magic which can be practised and presented on stage or in front of larger audiences at gatherings such as your local school concert or the Sunday-school party.

And there's those *mind-reading* and *memory tricks* (sorry, I've forgotten these already) – magicians call this *Mentalism*. Forecasting the football pools results a week before the matches are played is a form of prediction. We would have to be very clever if we wanted to do that, but it has been done in the past and very successfully too. Wish I could do it for I have always wanted to be a millionaire!

We mustn't forget the stunts and teasers which, although they baffle and con the customers, have no great skill attached to their methods or presentation.

A very wise magic man finds it necessary to dabble in all branches to achieve fame. His bag of tricks must be well varied if he wishes to succeed in pleasing most of the people most of the time. It means that he would have to select a number of varied *effects* (name given to tricks ... got it!) to form the final planned show. You can do the same using the tricks (sorry ... 'effects') described in this book.

Don't worry – my little magic people – Paul is here to guide you – not a lot ... but enough to show you that it is not only the secrets and the tricks of the trade which are so important, but the way in which you present them that really matters.

In no time at all you will become known as a magic man, one who baffles, bewitches and bamboozles his audiences and be the guest of honour at many important gatherings. You may even become famous! When that day comes, my friend, please don't be too shy to come up to me and say, 'Paul, mate – thanks for your help ... your book of magic was wonderful inspiration – it helped me along the road to success.'

PAUL DANIELS

1 Very Important Points on Learning Magic

Sit back – lugholes ready?

How do you like my book so far? What! Well, give me a chance, we've only just started and I have so many wonderful things to tell you, to teach you and lots of magical tricks to offer you. Look – if you don't like the book so far, chuck it out of the window, but do make sure the window is open.

That's better, so you like it, so take loving care of this book, for it is full of magical secrets.

And the first secret is for you to keep things secret.

Without secrets being kept secret we would never ever have anything secret. And the magic man always relies upon keeping his secrets *definitely* secret. It is so easy for him to divulge (tell tales) his secrets when his friends challenge him to do so. But the wise magic man should always shake his head and never reveal these. Once learnt, his secrets are his own and do not belong to anyone else, unless of course he or she has also bought a copy of this book of magic.

So, keep the secrets! If someone asks you – pleads with you – even goes down on bended knees, for you to reveal even one trick from the book – ignore the temptation, for you can always tell the person to buy a copy for himself. If he buys one, at least you will be satisfied to know that he *must* be interested in this wonderful world of magic.

The first important factor is that secrecy must always be adhered to. Without it, the magic man could not possibly continue.

The second, however, is something all magic men must do.

It's called practice.

In fact, all people in show business, even the top professionals, must practise their lines, their routines and their presentations before stepping on to a stage or appearing before television cameras.

Actors practise their lines for the play in which they have been given a part. Some parts are small and some large, but nevertheless a great deal of practice is necessary.

Jugglers and acrobats practise and rehearse their routines daily so that their act or complete show becomes so familiar to them that they could almost do it blindfolded. Some, in fact, *do* present their acts blindfolded, and even more care has to be taken when one is suddenly in the dark. A tight-rope walker, for example, could not possibly stop halfway while balancing on the rope to think what comes next. If he did he could be hanging around for days, months or years.

A person who plays the piano likes to play it well, of course, but would never dream of playing even a simple piece before an audience after only a few rehearsals. So, the magic man must follow others and do the same.

The tricks and stunts described in my book are all practical. I can show you that they all do work! To achieve the best results you must first practise the handling of the various items used and try to avoid making unnecessary gestures and movements. Don't for example hold something in your left hand and then transfer it to your right when it should really be in your right hand from the start. Audiences *do* follow hand movements very carefully.

Practise working the method of the trick, preferably in front of a mirror. Here, you will be able to see just how it looks to the audience. And please don't smile *too* much, for you might break the mirror and get seven years' bad luck for doing so!

It is only when you have mastered the workings and methods that you should try practising the actual *routine*. The routine is a term meaning the presentation of each trick. It also means that where a blended sequence has to take place, the performer must know how to link the various pieces together. Like a jig-saw, the right pieces must be made to fit where they belong. If you should lose a piece of the jigsaw, or disarrange it, you will ultimately be in trouble! We all make mistakes at one time or another, and the wise magic man must be experienced enough to get out of these unexpected wrong-doings. He must therefore learn *ad-libbing* and *get-outs* which enable him to complete the trick that first went wrong, so that his audience is not aware of the introduction of un-scripted material.

Patter is the term used by lots of show-business people, magic people included. The word means the actual lines spoken by the performer, during the show. There is 'straight' patter, the type which is best used should the beginner be inexperienced or not ready to embark on delivering material of a comic nature. 'Comedy' patter is that delivered by the magic man who wants a humorous type of presentation, so that he recites lines of joke-type material while he is performing his tricks. Comedy can also be introduced into a trick where patter is not used, and this is called visual or situation comedy. Sometimes called slapstick comedy, this brand relies on people who are able to mime or present comedy visually without patter or talk.

'Patter' is words, and often, words are so difficult to learn. (I am still trying to learn the English language – what's your excuse?)

But, magic people, never learn lines so that it appears that you are reciting them like a robot – after all, you are human (are you?): do try to recite them naturally. Never try to copy the styles of other magicians. If you do, you will always be known as 'Mr or Miss Carbon Copy', someone who should never exist. After all, who wants to be second best, anyway? No one!

A magazine reporter once asked me, 'Paul,' he said (that's my name, you know, must have been a clever fellow), 'what, in your opinion is the real secret of magic and being a real magic man?'

I looked the fellow up and down, and then down and up – he was so tall – and told him in one word ... one simple word. 'Entertainment,' I said, 'that's what all show business is about ... entertainment.' It is no use baffling and mystifying people all the time if you don't really entertain them at the same time. I have seen many clever magicians, over many years, perform very clever tricks and illusions, romping through their routines and presentations, offering a wide variety of effects, but somehow they never really seemed to entertain the public. Their tricks and illusions were beautifully made, presented nicely, but never made to entertain their audiences. So even the best tricks, even the classics when presented badly, without entertainment in mind, become disastrous pieces of equipment and the blame must fall on the performer. The audience may have applauded but they were not pleased or entertained.

Personality counts so much! Every one of us has a personality. We were all born with one. Some have more pleasing personalities than others. We are grateful to have what we have, but the wise magic man should first realize what his personality really consists of. It would be useless if, for example, he should practise presenting comedy tricks when he in fact hasn't got a good sense of humour. The magic man who wants to get laughs must let his hair down (no, silly – don't take your wig off, just let your hair down ... that's what I meant!).

Take *mentalism*, that area of uncertain things, and just think of how ludicrous it would be for someone to delve deep into this branch if they have only a rather timid sort of voice. 'Look into my eyes ... please,' are wonderful words when spoken dramatically by an actor or someone who has a deep and cultured voice. But the same words, delivered by a person who unfortunately has a very high-pitched, rather squeaky, tone becomes a farce. It is better for such a performer to use comedy as the theme, using a much lighter approach to things in general.

I saw a silly fellow the other day present what he thought was a very dramatic presentation of mentalism. He displayed a small slate and then started to open a packet of chalks. He couldn't get the top off the packet because it was the sealed bottom he was trying to open. When he realized this, he reversed the packet only to find that he had previously forgotten to close the lid. The chalks fell on to the floor.

He frantically gathered the chalks and replaced them inside the packet.

He was now in terrible trouble, and he knew it!

But he carried on like a true artiste, right to the end.

He finally did remove one piece of chalk from the packet but when he started to write the name of a chosen card upon the slate, the stick of chalk snapped and even the piece left in his hand turned to powder. It didn't seem to be his day. Even when he managed to chalk the name of the chosen card upon the slate's surface, he stopped, and, once again, realized that everything was not as it should be. He had actually divined the name of the card wrongly – a guess which went as sour as last week's milk!

Things like this happen to us all and I never like knocking anyone in particular, but this case does help us to make sure that it never happens to us should we be using similar materials. Believe it or not, the fellow who went through this terrible trial is a great friend of mine, a most accomplished performer and one whom I regard as being a dexterous magician. He handles his properties with great finesse and has made sure that things like this will never happen again.

No matter where you go, or who your audience is, you will always find those 'smart alecs' who know it all. They *seem* to know the secret of nearly every trick you present. Of course, most of them know very little, but they do often like to heckle, and try to spoil the show. A magic man, like a politician, if not experienced, can often be put off by an experienced heckler who keeps intruding and tries to make it difficult for the magic man to carry on.

Some time ago, I recall a member of my audience – a man in his late thirties, I think, definitely drunk – staggering around and shouting out, 'It's up your sleeve!' In fact the trick which I had just performed did not use the sleeve at all to vanish the coin I had displayed moments before. But this fellow kept repeating, 'It's up your sleeve.' I ignored him at first until he really became a nuisance to everyone. I pointed to him and said, 'Sir – I do hope you don't mind me calling you sir ... it's only in fun. Sir, please stand up against that wall over there – it's plastered as well!' The entire audience laughed, but now they were laughing at the fellow who tried to spoil the show. The tables had turned and he became the butt of the joke, so luckily he never really did get the chance to spoil the show. But this is only one isolated case. I never get cross or upset over silly things like this. Simply laugh them off, and make a joke of it all. If, for example, someone says, 'Seen it before,' say, 'So have I, that's funny, we've both seen it, so goodnight to you.'

One magic pal of mine always keeps a little impromptu reply up his sleeve. Well, to tell you the truth, not up his sleeve but within himself. If someone happens to shout out, 'Seen it on the telly,' you say, 'OK! So have I, but now you are seeing it LIVE!'

Performing before a public means that your hands are very much in view most of the time. Hands, fingers, nails and anything connected with them (well – your arm is connected to your hands) must always look clean, tidy and immaculate. It is truly amazing just how much dirt accumulates under your fingernails, and it is not surprising just how many of your audience will spot your dirty nails. Keep them clean. Trim your nails with scissors or clippers, making sure they are as neat as possible (makes you become a better magician too!), and in general, wash your hands thoroughly before a show, even upon arrival, so that dirt and grime can be removed instantly. I always remember an old lady telling me about a magician who presented an excellent show. 'What a lovely show, and wasn't he wonderful,' she said. 'Pity his hands and fingernails were not clean ... they offended me terribly!' The old lady is right, you know, for a magic man with filthy fingers is not a magic man at all ... unthinkable! (Who, for example, has ever heard of dirty fish fingers? No sir! Fish do keep their fingers very clean and tidy!)

Like your hands and fingernails, your appearance too should be clean and tidy. It should be immaculate. If you can afford to spend money on a special suit, such as a dinner suit with bow tie, you are lucky, but a lounge suit, smart necktie and a nicely laundered shirt will be most acceptable. Girls also look neat in a trouser suit or a dark, well-pressed dress. Please don't forget to polish your shoes. So often magic men do forget this important point, often forgetting that during travel shoes can often get dirty and will lack the shine they normally have. From top to bottom, your appearance should always be immaculate. Remember, please, that all eyes are upon you from the moment you walk on to the platform.

So – magic people, if you really do want to become a really good magician, please follow my advice. It's far better to be a good magician than just a competent one; try to be one who really knows what his audience expects of him. This means that you will ultimately enjoy performing magic and shows, and your audiences will appreciate your offerings all the more.

I hope the tips and hints I have outlined will help you in becoming a better magic man. Try them all, and if you don't like any, blame me. Blame yourself if you fail in accomplishing a certain trick, of course ... but not the magic I have to offer, for it has all been tried and tested, put into action at some time or another and proved very successful in my own hands. If you don't like any of the tricks I have described, please write your complaints in the space shown here.

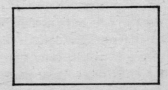

2 *The Magic Man's Table*

Most magic men perform their tricks on magic tables. Don't get me wrong – the tables themselves are not *magic* – they simply assist the performer to work more practically and form a decorative surface on top of which so many things can be displayed. Professional tables suitable for the magician can actually be bought. You won't find these at your local branch of Woolworths, though, for these are sold through magical dealers – people who spend a lifetime developing and manufacturing special pieces of magical apparatus and accessories for the magic man. But such tables are costly, perhaps too costly if you're just starting on your hobby and don't wish to fork out lots of money at this early stage.

The tables seem to vary in appearance. Some have four legs, but most have one. Some consist of tripod-legged tables, made from tubular steel, whilst others resemble suitcases so that when he arrives at the show, the magic man can press a button and turn his case into a perfectly practical table. A trick by itself, if you think about it!

But don't despair, magic people, you can still have a magic table of sorts even though you may be short of pocket money.

Possibly there is a table in your home that will do fine for this purpose and if you ask Mum nicely she may let you have it for special appearances. A small hall-type table, drawer-type table, or the kind known as a wine table, normally with a round top and one main leg to hold it upright, are ideal. Any one of these, suitably draped with a scarf or fancy cloth, will not only look very attractive, but will be most practical. Put the tricks you intend using on top of the table and you are halfway to becoming a real magic man.

If you are lucky enough to have a table which has a sliding drawer, use this in preference to the others. The drawer comes in very handy. Unwanted tricks, those which you will want but don't want after you have used them, can be discarded inside the open drawer, allowing you to have an uncluttered table-top. It's always terrible working on an untidy surface anywhere, the magician's table included. The drawer can also be used as a *servante*, the magician's term meaning a secret shelf or cavity that's hidden behind the table – secret things can be dropped inside without the audience knowing. It can also be used for

the magic person's table

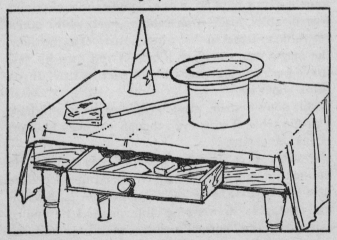

loading things into hats, boxes and other containers just as easily.

Here's a good example: A playing card or object which has been secretly palmed in the hand can be casually ditched into the open drawer, which, ideally, should be lined with cloth (a tea towel will do nicely), so that when the card finally falls, the cloth softens the blow. In other words, no one will hear it land – and that's very important! This also means that your hands are empty at the end of the trick.

A *servante* can also be made from cloth. In fact, the tablecloth which covers a card table can be used in this manner. Drape the table as normal but allow part of the drape to fold into a pocket towards the back of the table. Two safety-pins assist in securing the upper ends, forming a pocket. This open pocket becomes your *servante* where objects can be dropped in or taken out.

Ever seen a magic man produce lots of things from an empty top hat? Even a live rabbit? Yes? Well – usually he has used his *servante* to aid him in the production. You may not have a rabbit kicking about the house, but try it with another *load* (another magician's term meaning items to be produced).

Try it for yourself. Take a cloth napkin or large handkerchief and lay it flat on your table – before the show, of course, and in secret. Several objects are placed in the centre of the napkin, the four ends of which are gathered together, making a tightly formed bag bulging with goodies. Tie the corners around a large curtain ring and you have your load well and truly concealed within the bag. The bag is secretly hidden inside this pocket (sorry – *servante*) with the ring to the top, ready for your thumb to be inserted when the time arrives.

The top hat, with its opening downwards, should be rested on the table surface and positioned towards the back.

Lift it up, turn it over and look inside, telling the audience: 'This is a very big hat. Do you know who wears a big hat like this? Yes, a man with a big head. It's empty, as you can see, and I would like to produce a live rabbit from inside it ... ready ... ABRACA-DABRA ... HOKUS POKUS ... MYXOMATOSIS – sorry, wrong word, even to a rabbit's ear – and what's this we have inside the magic hat ... a rabbit ... no – not a rabbit – but a hare (hair).' Here a long brush hair is produced from inside, getting some laughs into the bargain!

'That's it ... I'll never ever be a magic man for I don't seem to be able to produce anything from the hat!'

The hat is replaced on to the table, opening downwards and towards the back of the table.

'Let's try once more – it's becoming old hat to me!' says the magic man.

The thumb of the right hand enters the curtain ring while the other fingers grip the rim of the hat. In one swift movement, the hat is lifted – not up – but hinged over from back to front, so that the hanging bag actually swings inside. To the audience out front, you are merely lifting the hat from the table and inverting it so that it is left mouth upwards. Your load is now inside! Reach inside and gasp with astonishment as though you just cannot believe your eyes! Something wonderful has just happened and you show it on your face by smiling. There's nothing like being enthusiastic about your own achievements!

Both hands reach inside and assist in opening the napkin bag, while a pretence is being made that you are getting ready to pull something out. Produce all the items previously placed inside and if you want to be really cheeky, pull out the napkin as well, as

the bag swings into the hat

part of the production. Now you *are* being clever, for not only have you miraculously produced many items from an empty hat, but have actually produced the 'load-bag' as well. Experienced magicians carefully load a real live bunny into similar bags and produce them from hats. Trouble is – they have to feed their load every day, and look after the bunny so that he not only finds it comfortable inside the bag, but likes swinging into the hat!

3 *Wanderful Magic!*

Every magic man has a magic wand. Without one, he could not possibly do his magic, for it is a very important piece of magical apparatus. I must own hundreds! Let me explain. Often, only *one* magic wand is in view during the show, but we magicians keep a few up our sleeves to bring about the most surprising of results.

There are magic wands which break into pieces, spin around, rise in the clenched fist, appear and disappear. And that's just a few which are specially made for a specific purpose.

These are specially made wands which are identical in size and colour and which are used throughout the show.

The magic wands that I own, and those which most magic men have in their bag of tricks, measure approximately 14 inches (35 centimetres) long by ½ inch (12 millimetres) thick.

It doesn't take very long to make one. The wand consists of a length of dowel rod, well sanded and painted black and white. In other words, a magic wand is a bit of stick. One magic man I know always makes a joke about this, saying, 'I'm a Mystic ... and here's me stick,' showing the magic wand as he recites the last few words.

Making Your Magic Wand

Buy, beg or borrow a length of dowel rod. Sand it down if you have some sandpaper, and give it an undercoat of paint. When dry, paint the centre black and the two tips, one on each end, white. Remember to put the lids back on to the paint pots and clean the brushes or Dad may become rather angry. Most of my furniture at home is somewhat covered in black and white speckles – untidy me!

Now that you have made your wand you will be wandering (wondering) just what you can use it for. Well, the magic wand is used for lots of things. It's mainly used for waving over things you intend vanishing, or over other *props* (theatrical word meaning properties, or objects used in stage presentations) you wish to appear, or change into something else or simply to change the colour of something to another.

The magic wand is also used for misdirection (Miss Direction? Who's she?)

Seriously though, magic people, without misdirection, we magic men would be out of a job. The meaning of the word is that here is the clever art of misleading the spectators' attention at the important

moment during a trick. For example, if you pretend to place an object such as a coin in your left hand, but really you secretly hold it in the right, and then bring the empty clenched fist of the left hand up, and peer at it, you are misdirecting your audience's attention. Their eyes will follow your hand movement as though the coin were really there inside, when in fact it is secretly *palmed* (concealed within the hand) in the right hand. Got it?

The magic wand can be used to point to things, using it again for misdirection purposes.

The wise magic man can also conceal something in his hand while holding the wand at the same time. The same applies to things which must be disposed of. When you hear a magician talking about *ditching* an item, he simply means he is getting rid of it secretly, without the audience realizing that this is taking place.

Here is one of the first tricks I learned using a regular magic wand.

Magnetic Wand

The magic man rubs his wand on the sleeve of his jacket. 'We have to introduce some LIGHT entertainment into the show, Ladies and Gentlemen, so I am going to make Electricity. May I introduce "Electricity" ... that wonderful pop group – wait – what am I talking about?' The wand is rubbed on the sleeve to make the pretence that electricity is the real secret of the trick when in fact it is not. The magic wand is placed against the left hand which is then turned over – and lo and behold – what do you think? It suddenly and most magically clings to his fingertips as though it were magnetic.

No – you don't need magnetic fingers to perform this trick, nor do you have to have a magnetized wand.

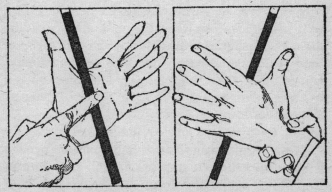

rear view   what the audience sees

And there's nothing sticky attached to the wand or to your hand, either! So there!

Here's how to do it. The wand is held in the left hand and reversed so that the back of your hand is towards the audience. The right hand assists in holding the left wrist firmly. In doing so, the index finger of the right hand holds the wand against the palm of the hand. From the audience's view it appears that the wand remains completely suspended against the left palm. Quite uncanny really!

Don't thank me for this clever trick – thank someone way back in 1860, who, whilst playing with a piece of stick one day, realized that this could be done. I was born later – much later (I think!).

Adhering Wand

Still using the magnetic theme (funny, though, for none of the wands actually use magnets), here is yet another very clever magic wand ... one which adheres to both hands when all the fingers are showing (look how we have progressed since then!).

A regular wand, made from dowel rod as previously explained, can be easily *gimmicked* (another fancy word magic men use when they talk about genuine pieces of apparatus being faked or altered to make things work fantastically), so that two small nails, painted black, do the work for you. These are knocked in – sorry, hammered – into the dowel rod, one at each end.

From the front, the magic wand looks genuine. But when the magic man wants it to become suspended between his hands, he uses the nails to assist him in this effect. Look at the drawing and note how both thumbs engage themselves on to the nails, both pulling on these so that the wand appears to be suspended. This same wand can be made to adhere to one hand. And in this case, only one nail is used so that it engages between the middle fingers of the right hand.

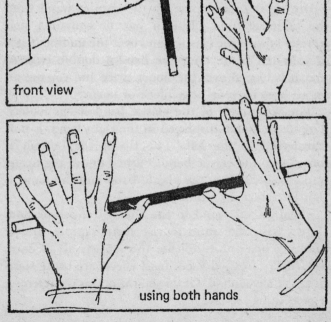

nail heads

front view

side view

using both hands

It stays there, suspended! Marvellous – we are certainly living in a magical world of make-believe!

Up and Up Wand

The cost of living, the price of this, that and everything you care to mention seems to be going up and up. So, magic people, cash in on the times and use the theme well for this next special magic wand. For, here is a regular magic wand which, when held in the clenched fist, rises, moves, and reaches the top of your fist. If you are looking for a rise, this magic wand will help you get it!

You need a fairly strong elastic band, plus the regular wand, of course!

During the show, pick up the regular wand from the table or from inside a box or container and secretly engage the elastic band over the middle finger of your left hand. Give the band a double twist so that it is looped over the finger twice and you are all set to present your next piece of magic.

The remainder of the elastic band hangs loosely. The magic wand, displayed in the right hand, is now transferred to the left. The tip at the bottom is forced into the elastic band. Pushed down, the magic wand is forced into the elastic band and the hand is tightly clenched around it.

To allow the wand to rise slowly, release tension. If you wish the wand to rise more rapidly, almost jumping up, simply release the tension all at once. Whichever method used, both effects are quite startling, as I have found. Or do you think this is stretching a good thing too far?

Smartie Wand

You won't find this version in any other book, for although it is based on an old trick, it really does look different from anything else now seen.

The magic man shows a small pay envelope and looks inside it (for his pay, I suppose). There's nothing inside. It's empty and contains – nothing (and you know what nothing is – a balloon without a skin!).

The magic man tips the envelope over an empty saucer and – PRESTO – lots and lots of Smarties or small coloured sweets pour out from inside it, dropping into the saucer. If that's not good, listen to what has to follow! The magic man tells his audience that it was all done with the aid of the faithful magic wand, and then proceeds to produce it (remember – 14 inches (35 centimetres) long) from the tiny envelope! The envelope is torn into tiny pieces, proving that it is quite unprepared. *Here's what you need.*

An ordinary pay envelope. A specially made magic wand. This wand is really made from a length of plastic or metal tubing, hollow right through, but capped at one end only using a piece of cork or something similar. Even a bit of chewing gum will do, but enjoy the flavour before using it for this purpose!

The tube is painted black and white and resembles a magic wand.

The envelope is prepared by cutting a hole in its back, just large enough for the wand to slide through.

The wand is filled with Smarties or other small coloured sweets, the more the better. These are carefully loaded inside, otherwise you may drop them all over the place and then you won't be so smart after all – you smartie artie!

The real secret of the trick is to have the wand hidden inside your left-hand jacket sleeve, so that the open end is towards the edge of the cuff.

All set? Let's start the performance!

Display the envelope and tell your audience that you went into a big store the other day and asked the girl behind the counter if she kept stationery.

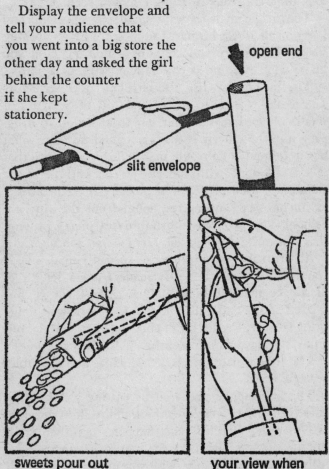

open end

slit envelope

sweets pour out

your view when wand is produced

Then tell your audience that she turned to you and said, 'Sometimes – but I often wriggle a bit!' Get it? And when the laughs (we hope) die down tell your audience that you asked her if she sold pay envelopes and she said yes, and display one which you supposedly bought.

'It's got nothing inside ... it must be the pay envelope meant for me! I've heard of people getting low wages, but this is ridiculous! Don't you think?'

The envelope is held in the left hand. The fingers of the right hand enter inside and grasp the open end of the wand from the sleeve, bringing it into the envelope. When the left hand is tilted over the saucer, lots of Smarties seem to cascade from inside. Here is the production of many coloured sweets from an empty envelope. Take your bow and tell your audience that it was the magic wand which made it all possible. From inside the tiny pay packet, pull out the 14 inch (35 centimetre) long wand and tear up the envelope. By destroying the prepared envelope you are thus destroying any fakery which otherwise would have been seen, if you should leave it lying around.

Melting Wand

Here's a magic wand that melts, dissolves and penetrates through matter and simply defies all laws of gravity. For example, you can push it through the middle of your little sister's tum! It won't hurt ... well not a lot ... but be sure to pull it out again or you will be in terrible trouble! The Melting Wand is harmless – it's as harmless as a fierce lion which has just escaped from his cage!

wand

hollow tip

The wand we use in this experiment (I call it an experiment because experiments *can* go wrong) is the same length and shape as the regular ones previously described. The only difference here is that it has only one white tip on one end.

You will also need an extra tip which is made of card or thin plastic, curled around so that, when stuck or taped, it forms the shape and can slide down the length of the wand. In other words, it is a sliding tip.

Have this extra tip on the wand, where the missing painted tip should be.

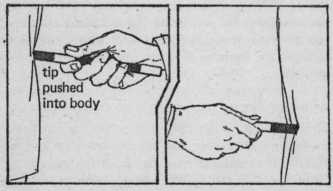

rear view   front view

tip
pushed
into body

The show is about to start and you are getting rather nervous. Stop biting your nails and put that chewing gum away. You simply cannot go on with a mouth full of chewing gum!

Display the wand, showing it around.

Ask for someone to assist, and if you can't find anyone, your sister will do fine. Tell your audience that you propose to push the magic wand through the volunteer's back. If you are lucky enough to find an attractive young lady from the audience do mention that it is a pity to experiment on someone so nice. If it's your sister, tell lies (she *can't* be nice, can she?) or perhaps the audience may think she is. Force the wand into her back and – not so rough ... OUCH – you bully!

Your right hand holds the far end of the wand while your left fist covers the sliding tip.

Both hands pretend to push the wand through her back. The left hand, concealing the sliding tip, brings it secretly up the stem of the wand and on top of the painted one.

The right hand pushes the wand and moves the sliding tip along so that it appears to be penetrating her back. The tip can be made to slide back and forth until you require the wand to actually penetrate her body all the way. The right hand starts to make the wand penetrate, melt, dissolve by pushing the hollow tip along to the opposite end. The remainder of the wand enters the open sleeve of the jacket or cardigan and from the front it *does* really appear as though the wand were melting through the young lady's back.

It's an optical illusion and one that works!

When the sliding tip is next to her back, the magic man can now reverse the procedure, by withdrawing the wand. The sliding tip is slowly drawn back until it reaches the opposite end and covers the painted one.

Don't let go of the opposite end, minus a white tip. Remove it from the girl's body with the left hand covering the untipped end and allow the right hand to rub the wand several times, moving the sliding tip back down to the other end.

Like it? I do! It's a miniature illusion using a magic wand and your little sister. If she won't help you, even though you have 'tortured' her, try the girl next door! You may even start to like her!

Now You See It – Now You Don't

For more years than I like to remember, and I can't really remember even a few months back, the famous Vanishing Wand was a great favourite amongst many magic men. Magicians have been vanishing magic wands long before we were all born, and that's a happy thought, my magic people, even if it is not the most important of news to come your way.

Here is a version of my own, and I have deliberately changed the ending of the original effect (clever me) so that not only has the magic wand vanished completely, but in its place is – yes – a string of beads, a nice gift for one of your girl assistants should you feel like being generous.

You already have a regular magic wand (or you should have, by now) and this is used together with an additional faked tube of black paper. Black poster paper or flint paper is ideal, or oblong strips of origami paper (black on one side) makes it possible. Roll such a piece around your regular wand and paste the edges so that a tube is formed. Don't use this for a pea-shooter, for it is not that strong! It has to be weak enough to be crumpled and torn when it is wrapped inside a sheet of newspaper. The black tube resembles the wand when two white end tips are plugged into each end. Pieces of dowel rod, painted white, will do admirably. Some magicians glue or paste tips into the hollow black paper rolls, just to be safe, so they don't accidentally fall out during the show.

But before you paste or plug the second tip into the tube, load a string of cheap plastic beads inside. You will find these will slide in quite comfortably and you can shorten the length of the string should these be the poppet-type. Remember to paste the second tip into place.

What have you got now, my magic people? A regular-looking magic wand, such as you would use

wooden tip — paper shell — wooden tip

during the show. But we know differently ... *wink wink ... nudge ... nudge* ... keep it quiet!

You will also need a piece of newspaper. That's something which is black and white and RED (read) all over. And if you intend borrowing a piece please remember to ask Mum or Dad first for it may be today's paper and both still might be wanting to read it!

Now that you have all the things ready to present the trick, start by displaying the magic wand.

Roll the magic wand inside the piece of newspaper, round and round, until you end with a neat package, and twist the ends just like sweet wrappings look like.

To make the wand disappear – suddenly crush the newspaper package between the hands. Break open the paper, somewhere in the centre (that's near the middle!), and from there, breaking through into the paper tube of the wand, you extract the string of beads. Remove them slowly, bringing these out almost bead by bead.

When you have finally produced the beads, crush up the paper and wand tube and casually cast both aside. The trick is over.

You have miraculously changed a magic wand into a string of beads. Congratulations!

4 The Magic Circle Card Trick

You don't have to be a member of the famous Magic Circle to be able to perform this trick, which uses nine cards dealt from the pack. But I'll bet you that if you were and you showed magicians this super card trick, they would be just as baffled as I was when I first saw it. I still don't know how it works – but it does! That's often the clever thing about magic – it sometimes baffles magic men themselves.

Borrow a pack of cards, or use your own if your audience trusts you.

Any nine cards are selected from the pack and dealt face down in a circle on the table.

Ask a spectator to point to any card and then, in a clockwise direction, count one ... two ... three ... moving to another card as each count is spoken. The third card is turned over. The spectator is asked to repeat the procedure, starting again anywhere around the circle, to count one ... two ... three ... so that the third card is always the one which is face downwards, ready to be reversed. He must always start to count on a face-down card.

If the spectator starts the count and ends on a card already face up, the game is finished and lost. The aim of it all is for the person to end with all the cards face up, leaving just one card face downwards. The magic man, can do it every time and also make the last card the one that the spectator has chosen.

The first part of the trick is very clever, quite ingenious in fact, so try it yourself, before reading the secret and method. You will find it almost impossible to reverse all of the cards without knowing the real secret. The second part of the proceedings is also so diabolically clever and simple that it is hard to understand just how it all works – but it does, every time!

All right, you've tried and tried and it fails every time. Go on, try another time. Like me, when I did not know the secret, I lost in every account.

Here's the real secret!

When the spectator has had his try, gather the cards together and fan them, faces to the spectator, requesting that he should select any one card. The chosen card is removed by the spectator and shown around. It is then to be replaced on top of the packet of eight cards held in the performer's hand.

It is here that the magic man secretly notices the card on the bottom of the packet.

The cards are cut several times (not shuffled). They are cut so that no matter how many times they are cut the magic man always knows the selected card because it is always next to, and right hand side to, the card which was previously on the bottom. Let us say, for example, the bottom card was the three of clubs. When cut several times, the top card, the chosen one, will always be to the right of the three of clubs, when you fan the cards to look at them. Make one last cut to bring the bottom card that you noticed to the top. In arranging the circle, the magic man starts dealing at 'one o'clock' and deals a complete circle.

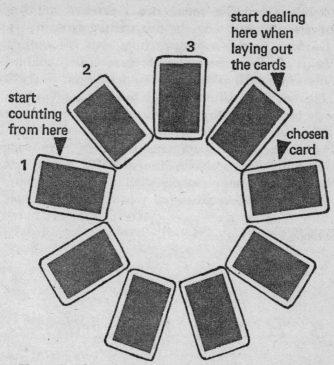

start dealing
here when
laying out
the cards

3

2

start
counting
from here

chosen
card

1

To make the trick work, so that you complete the circuit as well as end with the chosen card being the one and only card left reversed, start counting from the card marked 1 in the drawing. This card is pointed to and 'One' is called out. Working clockwise, the magic man points to the next card, counting this as 'Two' and the next as 'Three'. This third card is reversed and displayed face up upon the table.

The next move is a simple one, and this is repeated throughout until the circle has been finally covered.

Mentally count back two cards from your first starting position (marked 1 in the diagram) and commence counting clockwise, one ... two ... three ... and then reverse the third one, the first starting card, in fact. Go back another two cards from your last starting point and count to another three, reversing the third and so on until all but one card have been reversed. The last card, still reversed, is always the one which was first selected by a spectator, because whichever card you previously place at the second position within the circle always remains reversed. Try it for yourself and try to baffle Mum and Dad and the rest of the family. But please don't tell them how it's done, even if they threaten to put you into a terrible torture chamber. If they do – pretend it doesn't hurt! Oooooch!

5   Here We Are Together

Here is one particular trick which really does work itself. You won't even have to learn it, for there's nothing to learn. That's puzzling for a start!

A spectator is asked to shuffle a pack of cards and whilst shuffling to think of and call out two cards – only values and not the suits. These may be, for example, a five and a ten.

Deal the cards face upwards, one at a time, on top of each other – and, believe it or not, somewhere in the pack, when dealt or spread, will be a five and ten together. It works with any two cards and it is rather surprising to find that you don't have to be a master mentalist to achieve this feat.

It's always best to make your audience believe that you willed this particular prediction to happen naturally!

Remember, ALWAYS use a nice clean pack of cards.

6 All Fours

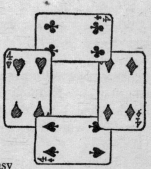

A puzzler, rather than a trick.

Ask a spectator to arrange the four fours of the pack so that only one of the fours printed on the corner of each card is left showing. Sounds easy at the start, but you will smile when you see your spectators try hard to fan and display the cards in a certain way – but always in vain!

But the experiment is definitely possible to achieve. You can do it if you know the secret. Anyone can do it if they know the secret, which I am about to tell you!

Arrange the four cards so that each overlaps, thus covering one of the index figures. The cards are displayed in a clockwise fashion and as shown in the drawing of how they should finally appear.

Clap hands – you've done it, Charlie!

NB Avoid those packs of cards with a number 4 in all four corners!

7 *Not a Lot –*
But What a Knot!

When is a knot not a knot?

When you're hanging around and don't know the answer!

When is a door not a door? *When it's ajar!*

When is a trick a good one, so as to puzzle your friends?

When it's like the one I am about to explain now!

Ask one of your friends if he can tie a knot in a length of string without letting go of both ends. Don't laugh when you see him try, for that wouldn't be fair. He obviously doesn't know the secret and hasn't yet seen a copy of my book. But when he does, he will see just how simple it all is!

Fold your arms before the trick and pick up the length of string.

Tie a knot. How? It's unbelievable, really, for when you pull your arms apart you will have a genuine knot in the centre of the string. One magic man I know did this trick and ended without a knot in the string, but instead found that he had tied a knot in his arms and just couldn't part them. Silly fellow!

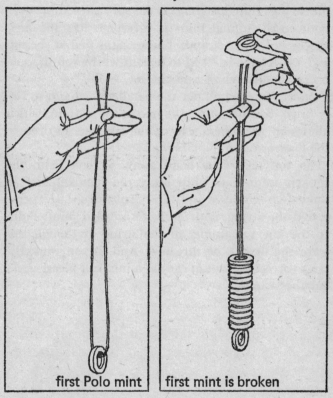

last Polo mint threaded on
to just *one* strand of cord

first Polo mint | first mint is broken

Here's a cute little trick which you can present almost anywhere. It uses those little mint sweets with the holes through their centres. Funny, I always prefer sucking the holes rather than the surrounding mint. I find them quite wholesome! Hope you like this trick.

Break open a packet of Polo mints and start threading them on to a length of string. The string is doubled up, and the first mint is casually threaded through one strand only. Thread another six mints or so down the string, but this time, make sure they drop over both ends. A final mint is threaded, like the first, simply down *one* strand. The string is tied at the top and a spectator is asked to hold it whilst you drape a pocket handkerchief over the lot.

Now, you reach under the handkerchief and secretly break the first mint, the one at the bottom, which allows all the others, except the last one, to drop to the floor or on to the table.

As you take your hand away, secretly palm the broken mint and whip away the handkerchief to show that all have well and truly magically penetrated the string, and the first threaded mint. Point to the one remaining on the string as though this were the first to be threaded. And, if you work the trick correctly, you can eat the mints, but please don't eat the string!

46

9 Find the Lady?

Where is she? Is she missing? No – of course she isn't.

But here in this trick, your audience sees the three ladies (queens) come together in a most unusual and magical way – and it is all so easy to perform.

Three queens are taken from the pack and one is placed on TOP. The second queen is placed on the BOTTOM of the pack. The third is pushed somewhere in the middle.

With a mere riffle of the cards the magic man shows that all three queens have come together and are indeed, there, in the middle of the pack.

The thousand dollar question is – how's it done? Well, I don't want a thousand dollars for revealing the secret of this super trick, but only thanks for passing it your way.

Have the four queens at the top of the pack.

Remove the top three cards (queens) and display them.

Place the first queen on TOP of the pack and the second on the BOTTOM. The third is placed anywhere in the centre of the pack.

When you cut the pack, thanks to that fourth queen which is always ready on top position at the start, the three queens come together. It's not the same three queens, if you think about it, for *one* differs, but performed quickly your audience will not realize that a fourth one was introduced to make the trick work.

10 Aces Traces

No – my magic people – it's not another name for a new magic spell. Aces Traces could well be that, but it is the name given to my next trick, one using a pack of regular playing cards.

Have the pack shuffled well and ask a spectator to assist.

He is asked to hand you the pack whilst your hands are held behind your back. Wait for it – you immediately pull the four aces from the pack and then hand out the cards to be examined!

The secret is so simple, so simple that even Simple Simon could do it.

Before the show, and in secret, remove the four aces from the pack. Have a small paperclip handy and a safety-pin. Fasten the four aces into the paperclip and link the safety-pin through the clip. Attach

four concealed aces

the pin under the back of your jacket, so it is out of sight, so that the four aces hang there, quite unseen by your audience.

In performance, and when the pack has been shuffled and held behind your back, you simply remove the four aces from the clip, one at a time, throwing them on to the table. The pack of cards can be handed to members of the audience should they wish to examine it. Tell your audience that you achieved this gift of finding cards by sense of touch. They may even believe you if you are good at telling lies.

11 'Mazing Matchbox

Just when Mum needs a match to light the fire, you can possibly assist her. But she probably won't like you one little bit when you proceed to open a box of matches and show it is empty – perhaps they have gone on strike! But, don't despair – there's magic in the air, for when you reopen the box, it is absolutely filled with real live matches. Mum will be pleased and may possibly give you an extra rise in pocket money for the week for being so clever.

To perform this trick you must prepare the matchbox so that it can either be shown empty or filled when the time comes.

Cut the inside drawer into two, right down the centre. Place both portions back inside the box.

Place the matches inside, and you are all ready to start.

When you perform the trick before the public, you must first pull out the inner drawer. Being only a 'half' drawer, makes it possible for the magic man to bring it up above the outer case and to all, it appears to be empty. Don't pull it up any further or you will definitely reveal the secret.

Push the inner drawer down, closing the box.

When you wish the matches to appear inside, you

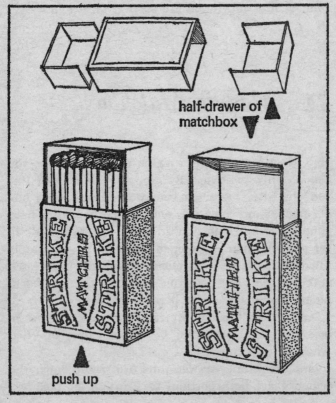

half-drawer of matchbox

push up

simply push up the inner drawer from the very base, so that both portions come up as one, at the same time, displaying the matches inside.

Tip out the matches so that the audience can examine them if they wish to, but please pocket the special matchbox. Better still, why not have an unfaked duplicate matchbox in your pocket, so that later you can casually bring it out and place it on the table just as an afterthought.

12 *Black and Red Mystery*

What's black and white and red all over ... a blushing zebra, of course – or could it be a sunburnt penguin?

What's red (read) – the daily paper, of course!

What's black – let's see – yes, a picture, a picture of a black cat eating a stick of liquorice, down a coal cellar, at midnight, in Blackpool. Don't believe me – simply listen to what happens in this following trick which uses both suits of cards ... blacks and reds! We don't actually use a pack of cards, though, yet the red and black mystery still exists.

You need a postcard and a black and red felt-tipped pen.

With both pens, you mark various card names, i.e. three of clubs, in black, of course, five of diamonds, in red so that the card displays nine such bold markings. The aim of the experiment is for the magic man to divine which are the red cards and which are the blacks when the paper is torn into nine pieces, and you can do this blindfolded.

The secret is very simple, so simple that when you learn it you will be absolutely amazed at the reaction it gets when performed before the public.

When you commence marking the postcard, start using the black-tipped pen. By starting with the black, it means that out of the nine markings which have to be drawn only four red card names are marked, these being scribbled in the four corners of the card.

When the postcard is torn into nine separate pieces it will be an easy matter for you to detect which pieces contain the red card names and which the black ones.

3 of D	8 of C	K of H
A of S	10 of S	2 of C
6 of H	J of S	7 of D

6 of H   7 of D

example: corner pieces displaying two complete edges

Behind your back, you have simply to feel for the pieces which have two complete straight edges, these being marked with red card names, the corners, in fact. The others, boldly marked with names of black cards, have ragged edges or only one straight edge.

So it is all done by feeling the edges of each piece. It doesn't matter how long you take to divine the colour of each, for you simply tell your audience that it was all done by 'mental photography'.

13 *Fly Away Peter –*
Fly Away Paul

This trick surely must have been named after me. It's one of the oldest tricks ever to be shown, and is wonderful for performing to very young children, for they all still seem to know the rhyme.

Two little dicky birds sitting on a wall,
One named Peter, one named Paul (that's me)
Fly away Peter, fly away Paul (off I go)
Come back Peter, come back Paul (now I'm back again!)

It's performed with two small pieces of paper.

The magic man sticks both pieces of paper (about the size of a half-penny) on to the nails of his index fingers. Use a bit of spit – or if you want to be correct, a little saliva from the mouth. Whatever you want to call it, this sticks the papers to your fingers.

Ready. Let's go!

Recite the rhyme slowly as you present the actions, for the pieces of paper represent Peter and Paul. Both disappear and reappear whenever you want, but always come back again!

Here's the secret!

Say: *Two little dicky birds sitting on a wall* ... Display both index fingers on the edge of the table, with the pieces of paper stuck to them.

... *One named Peter* ... Introduce him by tapping left forefinger on the edge of the table.

... *One named Paul* ... Do the same with the other index finger.

... *Fly away Peter* ... Raise the left hand up high

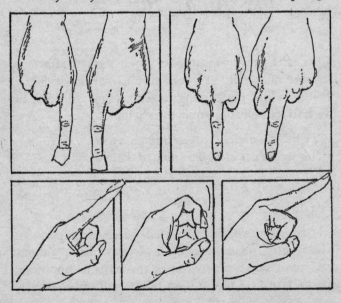

and as you do this immediately bring it back down with your middle finger on display showing that he has apparently gone!

Your index finger is curled into your fist.

... *Fly away Paul* ... Do the same with your right hand.

... *Come back Peter* ... Raise your left hand, changing over the fingers as you suddenly bring it down to show the paper piece has suddenly reappeared.

... *Come back Paul* (that's me) ... The right hand is brought down so that Paul reappears too.

The changing over of fingers may at first appear to be difficult to put into action, but I can honestly say that the working is as simple as the rhyme itself. This really is a trick to do for tiny tots. Sorry – can't stay any longer – must fly! Bye bye!

14 Blow Football – The Magic Way!

In every set of Blow Football you receive at least one straw and one ping-pong ball. Normally the player blows through the straw so that he forces the ball towards one end of the net, to win.

Here the rules are different! The magic man can show that his ping-pong ball (what a smell – what a pong!) can be balanced on top of the straw.

Not only this, but he can demonstrate the fact that the ball can mysteriously run from one end of the straw to another in a most uncanny fashion.

To perform this trick, you will need a straw, of course, and a ping-pong ball. Though those who play the game might insist you call it a table-tennis ball.

Before the show, secretly thread a length of thin white cotton through the straw so that its ends can be easily and neatly knotted together.

Use one of the ping-pong balls from your table-tennis set, and if you don't happen to have one, buy a single ball, for they are quite inexpensive. You don't have to buy the best grade to achieve this effect.

When you start the show, display both the straw and the ball. Tell your audience that both were taken from your very own Blow Football game and even demonstrate the antics of blowing through the straw

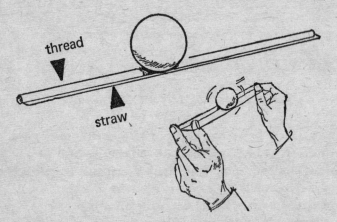

thread

straw

to show the audience that the ball shoots across the top of the table.

Your right hand enters the loop of thread, opening this out, while the left hand holds the ball, placing it so it rests between the thread and straw. The thread acts as a sort of rail for the ball to engage into and run along. When both hands hold the straw, the ball can be made to run freely from one end to the other, as though it were being balanced on the straw itself. It can be made to stop in the middle, jump up into the air, and roll off the straw whenever you wish.

15 Daylight Robbery

No, it's not really daylight robbery! The price of this book is the lowest we can possibly do it for, my magic people. Any lower and we would be giving it away!

Daylight Robbery is the name I give to this next card trick, and a most entertaining one too! If you don't mind me saying so. You do? – well, mind your own business!

It's the story of four burglars who plan to rob a big department store situated right in the middle of a big city.

The magic man displays their actions by using a pack of cards.

He shows the four jacks and places them in different parts of the pack. The story he tells ends as it should do so, with all four burglars (jacks) being caught, found together in the centre of the pack.

The trick relies on a cute patter presentation, and as you recite this the various moves are made.

You require a regular pack of cards, and this can be borrowed should you be performing the trick in someone's house. Before the show, and in secret, remove the four jacks and behind these have *three* more cards secretly hidden.

four jacks
plus three
other cards

You will find it quite easy to fan the jacks whilst the three additional cards are hidden behind, for when you fan to the end jack, you stop.

Place the four jacks (with the additional three cards) on top of the pack as you say:

'Four burglars, Ladies and Gentlemen,' (show the jacks) – 'these are four very modern burglars who planned to rob a huge department store which had four floors. They didn't start at the bottom of the ladder to work their way up, like most of us have to do in life. No – they hired (didn't steal it) a helicopter and landed it on the top floor of the building.' (That's the top of the pack when it is squarely stacked with faces downwards.)

'One of the burglars thought he would pop down to the first floor to see if the company safe was there, with the sole view of breaking it open and emptying its contents.' (Here the magic man lifts off the top card of the pack – really, an indifferent card – and places it on the bottom of the pack.)

'Another burglar used the mechanical staircase to get down to the second floor, which sold jewellery, to find out if there were any nice pieces to pick up!' (Here the magic man removes the next card on top and places this in the middle of the pack.)

'The third burglar secretly visited the third floor, selling the latest in ladies' and men's wear ... but didn't have much time to try anything on!' You must now remove the top card (third indifferent card) and place it somewhere near, towards the top of the pack.

'The fourth and last burglar decided to stay on the very top, to guard the roof and the helicopter and to look out for the police should they happen to come along.'

The card on top of the pack (really a jack) is lifted and replaced there.

'But something went wrong! One of the

burglars unfortunately set off the alarm system and, in no time at all, the police arrived in their panda cars and surrounded the entire building.

'The four burglars had a very clever idea. They thought that if they used the lift from top to bottom, they could perhaps get to the basement and make their get-away through a basement exit. They tried.' (The pack is now cut and the cut is completed.)

'But, alas, the lift jammed, and the police surrounded them all, and look – the four burglars are well and truly trapped in the middle.' (Fan out the entire pack and display the four jacks together.)

If you don't happen to like the actual trick, which I personally think is stupendous, then simply read the story. It may be the theme of yet another magnificent film in Technicolor, with a cast of millions (well – perhaps just a cast of four!), employing my trick and based on my offering called Daylight Robbery.

16 A Knotty Coin Trick

No – it's not possible to tie a knot in a coin, but this next trick is one which uses several old principles, but with a new slant, and perhaps it will baffle other magic men as well.

The magic man displays three different coins – a 10 pence piece, a 1 pence piece and a 2 pence piece.

He asks a spectator to select just one, and the one of his choice suddenly vanishes and reappears tied within a knot which suddenly appears in a handkerchief. That's magic!

How is it done, you may be asking yourself, and if you bend my little finger I will tell you, but please don't bend it too hard, please, for I am a little fellow!

Before you start and in secret, previously tie a knot at one end of a pocket handkerchief. Inside this knot, securely wedge a 1 pence piece. Place the handkerchief inside your pocket for the time being.

You will also need three other coins: a 10 pence piece, a 2 pence piece, and a duplicate 1 pence piece. On the back of the 10 pence piece, rub a small portion of soap so it clings to the surface.

Keep the side which has the soap downwards during the trick.

Arrange the coins in a row, on top of the table.

Now that you have done your homework, let's pretend the show is just about to start. You may be nervous ... not a lot ... but perhaps just that little bit.

The actual selection of the coin by the spectator is what we magic men call a *conjurer's choice* – no choice at all, in fact! The force, and it is a force, looks most convincing, and you can use this method to force lots of things.

Ask a spectator to point to one of the coins.

If he points to the 1 pence piece, that's fine, for that's the one you really wanted him to point to in the first place.

But if he points to the 2 pence piece, simply move

it away, discard it and say, 'Thank you – we don't want this one!'

Now try again.

If he should point to the 10 pence piece, say, 'And we don't want that either ... so, we are left with the 1 pence piece – congratulations!'

You have forced the spectator to select the 1 pence piece!

But there is another selection we must think about, before congratulating ourselves!

Should the spectator first point to the 2 pence piece ... discard it, stating that this is not required!

If he then points to the 1 pence piece, change

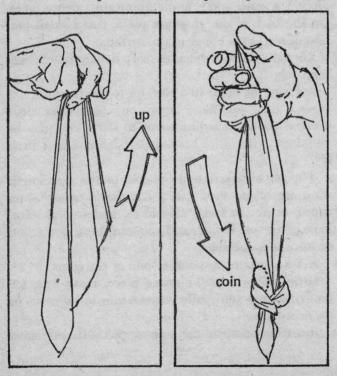

your patter and method, saying, 'From those two you have selected the 1 pence piece. Sir, the 1 pence piece you will have, and we will push the 10 pence piece to one side.' Whichever coins the spectator wishes to select, he has no real choice at all, for you, the magic man, have been able to cleverly arrange the coins so that the 1 pence piece is always left on the table.

Place the coins into your left hand, making sure that the 10 pence piece is carefully pressed on top of the 1 pence piece. The coins will stick together, the smaller one of the two adhering to the larger one. When you finally open your hand, the audience will see only two coins, the 10 pence piece and the 2 pence piece – the 1 pence piece having vanished completely. So much for the disappearance of the 1 pence piece – let us now consider the method of making it reappear in a knot which suddenly appears at the end of a pocket handkerchief.

Pick up the handkerchief, concealing the knotted end (which contains the duplicate 1 pence piece) in your hand.

Start to flick it upwards, pretending to tie a knot in it as you do so. After several unsuccessful tries, the knot suddenly appears on the end of the handkerchief. This is simply achieved by allowing the free end of the handkerchief to flick up into the hand so that the knotted end finally drops, coming into view. Suddenly, and most mysteriously, the audience see a knot appear on the end of the handkerchief.

Here's the real climax, for when the knot is finally untied, the selected (?) coin is now seen within it and is removed and shown. It's a super little trick and one that seems to amaze everyone.

17 Tricky Trap

I simply love swindles, although I hate being swindled! I like watching con-tricks and those safe bets which only the magic man seems to win in the end. I never use them to deprive people of their savings, leaving them penniless, but often perform them for fun. *Tricky Trap* uses a piece of string or silken cord measuring approximately 30 inches (80 centimetres) long. The ends of the cord are neatly tied together. This endless loop is twisted around so that a section in the middle remains open for a spectator's finger to be inserted. The magic man explains that either one of two things will happen. Firstly, should he pull the string, the spectator's finger could be trapped. Secondly, should he be lucky, when the string is pulled, the finger is free. It's a gamble, a game of chance and a chance for one of your spectators to join in on the fun! But please be careful, my magic people – don't repeat this swindle too many times during one show, for your audience may find out the secret!

The endless loop is brought over on to itself, from left to right (drawing 1).

When the bottom portion is brought over, a new opening comes into being, marked X. It is at this point you ask the spectator to insert his finger. It all looks so puzzling and quite impossible at this stage that even I have often wondered if it would work in the end. But when you pull the end loop it first appears to all that the spectator's finger will be

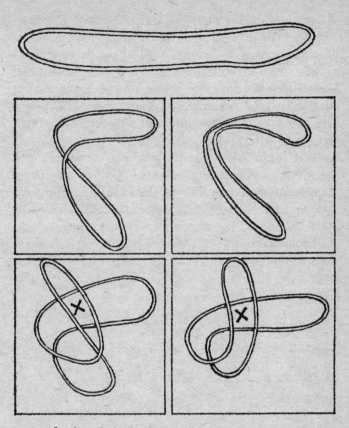

trapped – but it isn't, for somehow it always manages to get free.

Try and try again, using the same procedure, and you will find that his finger never seems to become trapped. Now, try for bets – but change the procedure. That's cheating, isn't it? Of course it is, magic people, cheating it is and please don't tell anyone – it's a secret, so don't even tell me!

The second arrangement of the loop of cord looks

the same as the first, but it is quite different. In bringing over this loop, the end is given a twist, then brought around as originally. The appearance looks similar to what you have previously demonstrated, with the same opening in the centre, looking most convincing, yet when the spectator places his finger into the same opening, and when the cord is pulled, his finger is trapped.

So it is possible for the magic man to either make his victim win or lose as the case may be, and if you happen to be playing for matchsticks, please do make sure you have lots of empty matchboxes, for you will need to hold all the matches you will ultimately win. As I told you, it's a game of chance, but one which you will always win. You'll never be out of matches — ever!

18 A Hole in Three

No, my magic people, it's not the game of golf which I am about to describe — it's a rather cute card trick which can be performed close-up and surrounded.

You won't find this particular trick in any other magic book, for this version is completely different. Let me tell you about it.

The magic man displays three playing cards. He explains that he has purposely made three holes in the cards, one in the corner of each, and these he shows to his audience. The cards are gathered together and threaded with a large wing-type paperclip. It seems impossible for anyone to remove any one of the cards from the clip, unless of course the card is deliberately torn.

The cards are covered with a pocket handkerchief and a spectator is asked to hold them by gripping the clip through the material. The magic man explains that he intends to remove the centre card invisibly, without the spectator feeling it leave. The magician pretends to remove the card, displaying it in its *invisible* state, and puts it (?) into his jacket pocket. The spectator is asked to remove the pocket handkerchief and check the secured fastener. It is quite secure – but wait for it – the card which was in the centre is missing – it's gone!

The magic man reaches inside his pocket and brings out this 'invisible card' and all three cards are handed out for examination.

Here is what you need to present the trick:

Four playing cards, preferably those taken from an incomplete pack, for you are required to damage the cards for this one presentation.

Better still, why not use a complete pack of cards simply for making up the various faked cards which have to be made and used in some of the other tricks I have described in the book.

The four cards consist of two regular pip cards plus two identical jokers.

A paperclip, the type with the flexible wings, is also required, and a pocket handkerchief.

The cards are prepared so the trick is an easy one to perform.

Before the show, place all four cards squarely together, so that the point of a knitting needle will bore holes in the left upper corners of all four. If you happen to own one of those small hole-punches, goody for you, for this will make an even better rounded hole in the cards!

With a pair of scissors or even a model knife, cut away a small portion of one of the jokers (see drawing).

shortened joker

dotted line shows
shortened joker

three cards
squared together

paperclip

Place the unfaked joker in your jacket pocket alongside the handkerchief.

Place the faked joker between the two regular pip cards so that when fanned, the three look quite normal. Make sure you don't fan the three cards so wide that the audience will see that the joker has a shortened side. In appearance, the joker simply appears as the central card.

With the paperclip near by, you are now set to perform this cute trick before the public – once you have learnt the various moves, of course!

'Ladies and Gentlemen, as a matter of fact this next trick demonstrates just how matter goes through matter, and for that matter, I want to emphasize the fact that matter through matter means solid through solid – just as a matter of fact, though. Well – what does it matter? I don't think it matters that much anyway! Ladies and Gentlemen – three cards ... Are you looking at the joker in the middle?' (No – not me – you silly magic people.) 'The one in the centre of the fan? He's the fellow who is going to be the real star of the show – not me, I'm only second best!

'You will notice, Ladies and Gentlemen, that all three cards have small holes bored through their corners, and if we knock the cards together – Knock, knock – who's there? Ivor ... Ivor who? I ver pack of cards over here – we can clearly see that all the holes line up.' This information is not only very educational, but quite useless, unless you are trying to learn the secret of this trick.

It means that the magic man can push the paperclip right through the holes in the cards. But when he knocks the cards up once more, the magic man makes sure that the joker with the shortened edge falls to one side, so that only those with the holes can be secured by the paperclip.

The handkerchief is draped over the set of three cards. A spectator is asked to hold the paperclip through the material of the handkerchief.

The magic man reaches beneath and carefully eases the joker card (which is not really securely clasped) so that it protrudes slightly from the other two. He then brings away his empty hand and displays the 'invisible' card, which he apparently pockets.

'What's that! You don't believe that the joker is invisible and that I held it in my hand? You don't! Well, I will prove you are wrong! Watch!'

The handkerchief is drawn away along with the protruding joker. The spectator cannot, in fact, feel the joker leaving the other two. The handkerchief, containing this faked joker card, is immediately pocketed, and the spectator is requested to have a further look at the remaining cards secured by the paperclip.

'Look, I told you – the joker is missing, and the other two cards remain securely fastened on to the clip. To release them you must first open the clip – please do that to prove this point, Sir. And where's the joker? – Yes – he's in my pocket. That's where I first placed him when he was "invisible" – but here he is, in reality.'

The unfaked joker is now removed from the jacket pocket and all three cards are casually left upon the table so that anyone who wants to can have a closer look. You may find a few will be looking for torn holes or faked cards, but you know, as well as I, that at this stage no such cards exist! Keep it a secret!

19 Three in a Row

Third time lucky – they tell us! Here the magic man not only reveals the third chosen card, but the other two. So, how's that for a hat trick!

Use a borrowed pack of cards and ask a spectator to shuffle them well. When the pack is returned to you, secretly note the card on the bottom – I mean the bottom of the pack, silly!

your first 'card'
to remember

Scatter the cards face downwards on to a table or on to the carpet. Don't lose sight of the bottom card, or you will be a dead duck.

Let's pretend that this card is the ace of clubs.

Invite a spectator to simply touch one of the cards, allowing him the choice of the pack.

Ask him to remove it slowly and concentrate on it, without looking at it.

Now, boldly state the name of the card.

Well, of course you don't know what card it *really* is at this moment, but you shout aloud 'Ace of Clubs' – the card you already know the position of.

Leave the chosen card face down and place it to one side, but glance at it as you do so. Ask another spectator to touch one of the other cards, and repeat the procedure, taking special care not to show its face at this stage. Tell your audience that this card is the queen of hearts should that have been the first card's name, and place it aside. Note the real name of the card as you put it to one side.

The magic man now changes the procedure. 'It's my turn now, Ladies and Gentlemen. I am going to select a card – let's see ... this one will do!' he says as he removes the memorized one, the ace of clubs. 'This is the seven of diamonds,' says the magic man, stating the name of the last card selected.

So, when all three cards are finally reversed, you will have proved that you are capable of 'mind-reading', for you have successfully divined the values and suits of the cards.

It's one of those impossible experiments which is definitely possible in the end!

20   *Ten Pence in every Bun*

The other day I was passing a baker's shop. It was very late Saturday afternoon and they were closing for their usual weekend Sunday break.

I poked my head inside the door and asked:
'Have you any fresh buns left?'

The baker smiled and said, 'Yes ... plenty!'

'That's your fault for baking so many,' I said, laughing. But the last laugh was on me, for I really wanted to buy one for the trick I am about to describe to you all, and thought he might not serve me. But the baker was a kind fellow and sold me a bun.

Now for the trick. The magic man displays a bun and places it in full view on to a saucer which a spectator is asked to hold.

He next borrows a 10 pence piece and has it marked, either by a pen or knife (cutting a secret mark across its face), so that the spectator who loaned it, will recognize it later (we hope!).

The 10 pence piece is placed under a pocket handkerchief, another spectator assists by holding it through the cotton material.

Abracadabra – Hey Presto – Hokus Pokus – Sizzling Sausages, the spells are recited (they don't really mean a thing, but they sound good). The handkerchief is suddenly whipped away showing that the coin has mysteriously vanished into thin air.

The magic man takes the bun from the saucer, breaks it open, and displays the same 10 pence piece inside – complete with its original markings. Since it belongs to the spectator, it is handed back, giving him or her lots of time to examine it thoroughly.

Here's the recipe:

You need one bun. Bake it yourself, pinch it from Mum's cupboard or simply do as I did, buy one from the baker's shop down the road. Buns are not all that expensive – they don't cost a lot of dough!

You also need a saucer, a pocket handkerchief, a piece taken from a similar handkerchief, cut into a triangular portion, and a certain amount of nerve. To prepare the pocket handkerchief, first place a 10 pence piece on to the corner, and with contact glue stick the additional portion over this so that a self-contained pocket is obtained. The 10 pence piece is trapped inside. Alternatively and possibly better in the end is for you to ask Mum to sew this additional piece on to the corner of the handkerchief.

Either way, the 10 pence piece is sealed inside the corner and is out of view.

Now, let's start the trick.

After the bun has been displayed and placed upon the saucer, let a spectator take charge of it. Make sure he doesn't scoff it up during the presentation, or that will be the end of a wonderful trick!

Ask another spectator to lend you a 10 pence piece, but request him to mark it in some way so that he will be able to recognize it later. A secret mark from a pen or pencil is fine, but a notch scratched on to the coin's surface will do even better. Take this coin from the spectator.

From your pocket remove the handkerchief, displaying it on both sides.

Drape the handkerchief over your clenched fist,

allowing the secret corner pocket to hang freely. The borrowed 10 pence piece is placed under the handkerchief. At the same time, get hold of the faked corner and bring it up inside the handkerchief, and ask a spectator to hold the coin through the material. Of course he holds the one trapped inside the secret pocket, while your right hand, palming the original 10 pence piece, comes away and keeps it there.

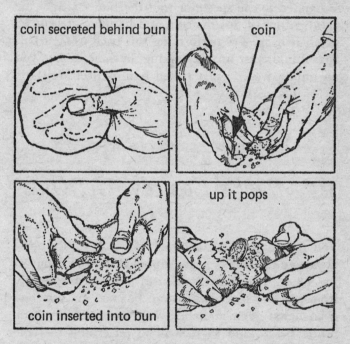

coin secreted behind bun

coin

coin inserted into bun

up it pops

Pick up the bun from the saucer, using your right hand, and bring the concealed coin beneath it. Your left hand reaches for one corner of the handkerchief, whipping it downwards, rather dramatically. Your audience will be completely astonished to see that the coin has apparently vanished (as I do often). But don't despair – Paul is fair! Both hands bend the bun, *upwards* at first, making the first break. The fingers of the right hand slip the coin into this break and when both hands bend the bun *downwards*, and then *upwards* (again), the coin always seems to pop out into view. The borrowed coin is definitely seen to be lodged within the bun, and when removed it is handed to the spectator (not the bun – silly – the *coin*). After all, it's his coin and he must at least be given it back. Try performing this trick using a borrowed bun. Just imagine asking someone to loan you an unprepared, freshly baked bun or bread-roll!

21 *Paul's Comedy 'Get-Outs'*

You may find, as I sometimes do, that things don't always go the way they are supposed to, when appearing before a public. Audiences differ tremendously from place to place, which can be good or bad. The good news: New audiences will not have seen your magic before and so it will be refreshing to their eyes. The bad news: You may be showing the same tricks before the same audience over and over again, and they often look out for those careless moves which perhaps didn't happen on first showing.

But who on earth would wish to perform the same

tricks before the same audience repeatedly? No one in their right mind – I guess!

That's why the wise magic man should always have something up his sleeve (no – not really up your sleeve or jersey) in case something goes wrong during the show. Indeed the comedy by-play and gags described here may also be used between the tricks you intend performing.

So – if a trick happens to misfire, or worse still, you suddenly forget what to do, and what comes next, break into the wonderful world of comedy and use some of the following visual aids.

A Quick Card Trick

From a regular playing card case the magic man removes the pack – but what a laugh when he says, 'Ladies and Gentlemen, I would like to present a little card trick.' Imagine the audience's reaction when the magician

removes a miniature top pack of cards from this large-sized case. It looks so funny!

Feeling Funny

During the magic show the magician removes a lighted candle from its holder and begins to eat it – bit by bit. Your audience will find it hard to swallow, even if *they* are not eating it!

The secret is that the candle isn't really a candle at all. It's a replica made from a long banana which

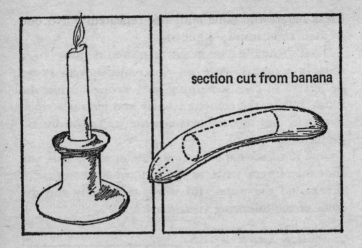

section cut from banana

has been carefully trimmed into a cylindrical shape. Into one end stick a slither of almond or brazil nut which acts as the 'wick', which believe it or not, can be lit.

Display the 'candle' in its holder and before you start eating it, remember to blow out the flame. Then surprise your audience by devouring it, gulp by gulp.

A much shorter candle can be made from an apple which has been likewise shaped.

Funny Matchbox

By cutting one end away from the inside drawer of the box, and loading the matches inside, yet another funny bit of business comes to light.

When the spectator starts to open the box at your request, all the matches suddenly fall on to the floor. Watch his face when you smile at him!

Bouncing Hanky

'It's hard work, this magic business – phew!' says the magic man, as he removes his pocket handkerchief and rubs the sweat from his brow .'That's better,' he says as he throws the handkerchief on to the floor. Somehow it suddenly and most surprisingly bounces into the air, where he catches it and pockets same. What a laugh!

To prepare the special handkerchief, fasten a rubber ball on to the centre with glue. When thrown to the floor it will automatically bounce back up into your awaiting hand. It's as easy as that!

Dead Match

Whenever you intend using a match to set fire to a piece of paper or even in offering a light to someone wanting to smoke, try introducing this funny novelty. It's a specially made match converted from a real one. Simply cover the normal match head with plasticene for a moment while you burn the stick beneath, using another match for the purpose. Don't allow the matchstick to burn right through, otherwise you will end up with a burnt-through matchstick. Remove the plasticene, apply glue on to the head and dip this into some cigarette ash which you will find in an ashtray. Now your special match looks like a real spent matchstick. Casually drop it amongst the other real spent ones, but do be careful, magic people, keep track of it, otherwise you will be in trouble.

Look for matches, but pretend there are none around, and then decide to look in the ashtray. Pick out this special one amidst the others and strike it against the matchbox surface. Just watch their faces when you seemingly strike a dead match only to make it light once more.

matchhead
covered

dip into
ash

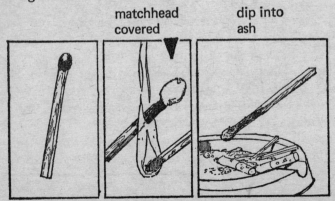

22 Any Page . . .
Any Word . . .
Anywhere !

I fooled an entire Chinese audience the other night by presenting this wonderful trick. They didn't understand a word I was saying and perhaps that's why I fooled them. The whole trick relies on words alone, but not Chinese ones.

The magic man hands a spectator a dictionary, asking him to turn to any page of his choice. When he does this, he is further asked to mentally count down to any particular line on this page, e.g. thirteenth line down, and then remember a word or words, or indeed the entire line should you so wish, and memorize it.

The magic man is able to suddenly announce the word, the words or the complete line, whichever the case may be. Your audience will be not only surprised but flabbergasted over the final result, and if you play your cards right, you will become a master mentalist almost overnight. But you will have to practise the presentation very carefully to achieve a certain amount of dexterity.

Like most of the best things in life, the real secret is so simple, and it is the actual presentation and showmanship gestures which ultimately count in the end. Remember, magic people, you can buy the most expensive piano in the entire world, but not be able to play it, or even play it well enough to be called a pianist. The same applies to the magic man, who, given the tools of his trade (tricks and secrets), may be able to *do* them adequately, but not well enough to perform before a demanding public.

You will need one piano (sorry) ... I mean one dictionary. Keep it a secret – you will actually require two similar ones, pocket editions, to make this experiment possible. Since these are called pocket dictionaries, these can be easily pocketed and this is what is done with one of the two.

The second, and indeed, the *only* visible dictionary, is on view during the experiment. Display it freely and do not go out of your way to call it a 'pocket dictionary'. Don't give your audience that chance to use their brains to realize that such a book is pocketable (I hope there is such a word as 'pocketable' for I like it – not a lot – but I like it!).

Want to know the real secret of this trick? *Pssst!* – keep it quiet, otherwise the entire country will know the secret.

Before the show, and in secret, place the second dictionary inside your jacket or trouser pocket.

When you actually start your performance, smile ... that's always a very good start, but don't be too false, for it never pays – just be natural! But a smile does increase your face value! Simply pretend that a piece of cheese has accidentally got lodged inside your mouth, so both jaws are wide open. OK ... wait a moment – I'm just finishing this lump of cheese! – that's better!

Hand the dictionary to a spectator, requesting him

to turn to any page he wishes, and he has a wide choice – the entire contents, in fact.

Ask him to glance at the page number and then at any line on this chosen page. Request him to concentrate on the word, on that line, on that page.

Retire from the room and behind the door shout out, 'I am thinking of a page number ... what number are you thinking of? I am thinking of a line ... think of yours, and please tell me which line from the top of the page you are thinking of?'

When the spectator reveals his selected page number and the number of lines down on that particular page, the magic man simply removes his duplicate pocket dictionary, opens it at that page and glances to the line in question.

Pocket your dictionary, enter the room and memorize the selected line. But the magic man doesn't really want to reveal words from thousands as simple as reading next week's grocery list. He wants to be much more subtle and clever than that! Slowly and dramatically, he reveals the chosen words and finds that he is fast becoming a remarkable mentalist.

23 A Printer's Dream Come True

Here's the magic way of printing plain and blank cards so that they finally appear as a fully printed pack of playing cards. One moment they are white and shining bright, the next they are printed. Here is the latest printing process which doesn't involve inks or mess or, indeed, presses! It's all done by magic.

The magic man displays a fan of cards, each and every one completely blank. He does, however, show the audience that the cards have a very attractive back design.

He gives the cards two taps – one hot – one cold! (Hot and cold taps ... get it?). When the cards are reversed, the entire pack is now fully printed on their fronts, all suits – all values! It's a wonderful trick.

In fact, this trick, so I am led to believe, was invented by that great Chinese magician Hung Wun. His brother was Hung Too! And I think I should be hung just for telling you such a terrible joke!

You lucky magic people, all you need is a regular pack of cards. You will have to make a special card, one that aids you in the printing effect. Use the joker (there's always two in every pack) and cover its face with either white paper or fablon contact material. You now have a blank card.

This card is placed on top of the pack, which should be face up.

The secret – yes! Most people fan a pack of cards from left to right so that all the faces, pips and indices are in view. Try reverse-fanning the pack, from right to left, and you will see a most surprising result. Most cards have their indices printed on two adjacent corners, so that when the pack is reverse-fanned in this manner, and not fully spanned, all the cards look as though they are blank. The unprinted edges assist in giving this impression, and because the blank card is on top of the pack the illusion is created.

normal fan   reverse fan

'Ladies and Gentlemen – 52 pieces of blank card. The backs have been printed but the fronts are still waiting to have their suits and values added. Let me show you the magical way of printing a complete pack of cards – from ace to king and all suits. Come to think about it, wish I could produce a new suit for myself, as this one doesn't seem to fit me lately!'

The magic man reverses the pack, fans it out, showing the back design on each card. 'Nice design, this – don't you think? If it were wallpaper, I would have it in my bedroom at home.'

As the magic man patters, he removes one or two cards and shows the back design again, making a point of replacing the top card (the blank-faced one) on to the bottom of the pack.

'Ladies and Gentlemen – please relax – just sit back and let your hair down. No, Madam, don't take your wig off, just let your hair down – relax and watch!'

Turn the pack over and fan the cards normally, from left to right. It's magic! A complete pack of printed cards. Please be careful not to show the end card which is the only real blank amongst the others. But, if you like, you can finish the trick by saying: 'Fifty-two playing cards, all fully printed and – sorry – no joker.' For (remove the blank card and display it) he's gone! 'Guess I'll have to take his place, good-night!'

24 A Hair-Raising Trick

I told an old man that when I did this next trick it would make his hair stand on end. I was wrong – because when he took off his cap, he was completely bald. You can't win 'em all, can you now?

Listen, magic people, it's creepy – it's crawly –it's a little miracle – enough talk about me and let's get on with the trick!

The magic man removes two matchsticks from the box and displays them freely, holding them between the finger and thumb of his right hand. He plucks two hairs from his head (only pretending, of course) and hands them to two spectators (and don't they look daft holding invisible hairs!).

The magic man asks both to tie the hairs around the tops of the matches and then not to let go the opposite ends. 'Pull on the hair,' says the magic man, 'pull, very, very slowly!'

Both spectators oblige and do just this, pulling on their invisible hairs. Suddenly, both matches seem to move, part and arc away from each other, in a most uncanny fashion. Is it realism, spiritualism ... or is it just trickery, folks? No, not now, not ever – it's magic, for both matches are immediately handed out for thorough examination and the spectators are allowed to keep the invisible hairs as souvenirs.

Here's the secret:

From a length of rubber bicycle valve-tubing, cut a 1 inch (25 millimetre) length. Force both ends of the matchsticks into the tubing so they are tightly wedged. You will find that when you bring both matchsticks upright, holding them between the thumb and forefinger of the right hand, they will appear as normal single matches. But when you gradually release the pressure, the matchsticks slowly part, thanks to the springy material used in the making of valve-tubing. The funny business of pulling two long hairs from your head creates further amusement and laughter,

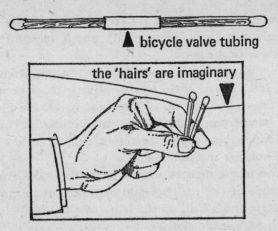

▲ bicycle valve tubing

the 'hairs' are imaginary ▼

and when the spectators pretend to tie their ends on to the heads of the matches, the audience often get quite hysterical, to say the least. When I performed this recently in front of an audience, one old lady laughed so much that she fell over and died. Mind you, she was almost 180 years old at the time.

When you wish to hand the matches out for examination, pull them out and away from the tubing, which is then concealed in the hand and secretly pocketed later.

Although valve-tubing is still available in the shops, it is becoming somewhat scarce. A good substitute, which works just as well, is a piece cut from an empty biro refill. This flexible plastic tubing works wonders when put to magical uses and could become your 'pen-pal' for years to come!

25 Separating the Reds from the Blacks

This next trick can also be performed with a borrowed pack.

The magic man tells his audience that he is able to tell which cards are red ones and which are black, when they are lying face down and spread over a table.

'It's all done by weight, you know – for they make the red cards heavier than the black ones – and that's how I tell the difference,' he says convincingly.

'Funny, really, for normally I can't tell the difference between butter and margarine.'

True enough, the magic man lifts each card, weighs it up and down on the palm of his hand and then reveals the colour – red or black. He can also state whether or not it is a light or heavy card and much fun can be had going through the entire pack, introducing amusing antics. The operation is speeded up and the magic man announces the colours of the cards in a quick fashion.

The secret is very simple – very simple indeed!

Before you do the trick and in private, separate the red cards from the blacks. Bend the black cards upwards and the red ones downwards and shuffle the entire pack so all the cards are well and truly mixed. Now it is time to perform the trick.

The cards are spread face downwards on to the table.

upwards

downwards

It is an easy matter to locate the reds and blacks because of the ways they bend. If the card you touch bends upwards, it's a black one. Downwards, the bent card is always red.

But please don't simply say, 'That's a red one and here's a black one.' Use the fascinating weighing theme. Pretend to weigh each card on the palm of your hand before announcing the colour. Don't be afraid to repeat black after black, but then change the pace so that the cards alternate red and black.

About halfway through the pack, quicken up the procedure by working fast, otherwise you will start to bore your audience, and you should never bore your audience – I should know (not meaning that *I* bore my audiences, but that I know I should never bore my audience).

Incidentally, you need only bend the cards *slightly* and at the close of the trick, gather them together and bend the pack downwards, so that all the cards will be the same and that the secret will not be spotted.

Anyone want to play cards with me?

26 Cut and Restored
Pyjama Cord

Here's a trick using a length of rope or cord. If you
don't have any, sneak into your brother's bedroom
and pinch his pyjama cord, but put it back later, so
that he will not notice when it's time for him to go
to bed. So, magic people, I won't want to receive lots
of letters from your Mums and Dads telling me how
you borrowed your brother's pyjama cord one night
and presented a show at your party the next – they
will recognize it!

Take the pyjama cord and fold it so there becomes
a middle – that's somewhere in the centre – of course
it is, silly!

Cut the cord through the centre and normally you
would have a wasted pyjama cord. But the magic man
cuts the cord, trims the ends and, surprisingly enough,
restores it to its full length.

The secret of this trick relies upon an extra length
of cord. If you don't feel you want to cut brother's
pyjama cord, you can use a soft rope. You need a
long length plus a short 6 inch (15 centimetre) piece.
Hide this extra piece inside a hat or behind other
items already on the table, so it is not seen by the
audience.

Have a pair of scissors beside it, for you will be
needing these later.

When the time comes for you to present the
trick, pick up the long length of rope and display it

to everyone. Let your audience examine it if they want to, for you have nothing to fear, my magic friends. The length of rope is as innocent as I am – well, almost!

Find the centre of the rope and let both ends hang downwards, drawing attention to the looped end which is then pulled through your clenched fist. Your right hand reaches for the pair of scissors and brings these into view, at the same time concealing the extra piece of rope, formed as a loop, with the same hand.

The long length of rope is transferred from your left hand into your right, while your left hand takes the scissors, but leaves the extra loop behind. It is this extra loop which is brought up through your fist. Magic people – you have just added this extra piece on to the end of the real one.

cut through extra loop

It is through this loop that the blades of the scissors are placed and then finally closed, cutting it into two. At this stage there appear to be two separate lengths of rope. Don't forget to trim the bits (cut loop) so that all of this loop falls to the floor, getting rid of it completely.

Blow on the remaining piece of rope, open your hand, and reveal that you have successfully restored the length of rope.

It's a great trick. It's Thuper!.

27   *Magic Dice and Dominoes*

Anyone for a game of dominoes? No – well, then, let's play with some dice. Better still, why don't we play with both and fool your friends at the same time?

All you need is a complete set of dominoes and two dices (sorry, I did mean to say – two dice).

A spectator throws the dice and notes the numbers on top, e.g. a six on one and a three on the other. The magic man presents the spectator with the set of dominoes and asks him to play a game on his own, matching each as he goes along. This he does. But before he starts, the magic man mentions that his game will end with his selected numbers – six and three spots. Remarkable – that is, if it happens, and it happens every time!

When completed, the spectator's game displays that the end dominoes are a six and a three spot.

How to do it? Here's how!

Have the set of dominoes, faces uppermost, scattered over the table or floor. Both dice should be near by.

Ask a spectator to throw the dice freely and point to the numbers which come up, e.g. a six spot and a three spot. Now display the dominoes and move them around, spotting the position of the one which carries these numbers. Secretly palm it while you mix the dominoes and pocket it later.

No matter which dominoes are played and in which order, the end ones will *always* display the same numbers as the one which was first stolen away. And remember, too, these are also the spectator's chosen numbers, taken from his dice throw. It's all so puzzling – so puzzling that I want you to get the set of dominoes out immediately and try it for yourself! It works every time.

This particular trick can be repeated over and over again, using different spectators to throw the dice and play the game of dominoes.

Now that we are left with two dice on the table, let me explain a little favourite of mine. It's rather clever!
I call it:

Dice Prediction

Scribble the number 14 on to a piece of paper, but don't let the audience see it at this stage. Fold the paper and let another spectator hold it. Call this your 'prediction paper', and explain to everyone that it will be read out later.

Ask another spectator to throw both dice upon the table and then to add the bottom number to the top of both dice. Funny – the answer is *always* 14, no matter how the dice are thrown. This is simply because the tops and bottoms of all dice always total seven. So, by using two dice, the total is definitely going to be fourteen.

One magic man I once knew used six dice to achieve the same effect, with the grand total of forty-two. Think I'll stick to two, one taken from my snakes and ladders outfit, the other from my Ludo!

28 *Snip!*

I could have called this next skilful-looking feat 'Snap' – but if you want to argue, let's call it 'Snip-Snap' just to please everybody! It's not really a trick, although it has a secret.

A spectator cuts a strip from a piece of newspaper and hands it to you. You throw the strip of paper up into the air and grab the pair of scissors in your right hand. Lunge forwards – and SNIP – you've done it! Done what? You may well ask. You have managed to cut the paper into two bits while it quickly floats to the ground. How's it done? Thought you might ask! Thought you would never ask! I'll tell you anyway!

It's all so very simple.

Before the show, and again in secret, wedge a small strip of newspaper between the blades of the scissors you propose using. The scissors have only to be partly closed to keep this portion in place. The broader the blades of the scissors are, the better, for obvious reasons, but this will not mean that you will have to scout around looking for the biggest pair of scissors ever made!

Now that you know the preparation, let me tell you how to work it! It's so simple that even the scarecrow out in the fields near by where I live is doing it, and getting applause!

Hold the strip of paper in your left hand – high!

Your right hand holds the scissors, with the hidden strip of paper, well concealed. The left hand allows the paper strip to fall and flutter to the floor.

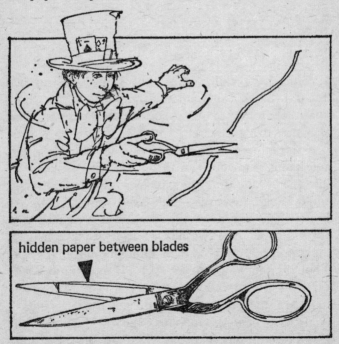

hidden paper between blades

But, magic people, when it starts to drop downwards (it's difficult to imagine it dropping upwards!) and about halfway, the right hand reaches forward and snips the blades of the scissors. The snipping sound is rather realistic and the concealed strip of paper falls to the floor as the blades are opened. It appears to the audience that you have cleverly managed to snip a piece off whilst it was in transit.

Try doing this amazing stunt the correct way, without using the extra piece of paper wedged between the blades of the scissors – and you will find it is almost impossible. Let your friends try the honest way – over and over again so that they will always fail.

29 *The Perfect Date*

Here's a nifty coin miracle using a dozen or so coins which are dropped inside a hat or container during the show. Everyone sees that all twelve coins bear the same date.

An additional coin, one bearing a different date, is shown and passed around so spectators can check this is so. The final spectator, holding this coin, is politely asked (civility costs you nothing!) to drop it into the hat with the others, all coins then being shaken within.

The magic man reaches inside the hat and immediately produces the coin bearing the different date. Only thirteen coins are used and the hat can be a borrowed one.

You don't have to be rich to perform this trick, but you will need thirteen pennies, twelve of these bearing the same date. The thirteenth has a different date and it should be inside your trouser pocket. The twelve coins should be kept inside one of your jacket or overcoat pockets, the garment in question being casually left outside in the hall, before you enter the lounge.

The whole secret – and nothing but the secret – is that this additional coin, to be added later, and inside your warm trouser pocket, will absorb a certain amount of body heat to aid you in the working of the trick. The coins which are inside your jacket or overcoat pocket, outside in the hall, will not be so warm (are you getting warmer? Thought you would be, by now!)

last coin is the 'warm' one

During the show the magic man tells his audience that he has a good trick to show them, and retires from the lounge to obtain the twelve cold coins from outside. He brings these back into the room and places them into a borrowed hat or container. He does, however, allow his audience to examine them, and in particular draws attention to the fact that all have the same date.

The thirteenth coin is taken from the trouser pocket and shown to bear a different date to the others. It is tossed into the hat and shaken up with the twelve other coins.

Although the coins are well mixed, because the thirteenth coin has been in a warmer place, it can be located amongst the others at a simple touch. So the magic man can reach inside and immediately bring out the coin bearing the odd date.

It's better performing this particular trick during winter months, for one reason or another!

30 *Magnetized Cards*

Just imagine! You are at a party and the host or hostess asks you to do a trick for the guests. You don't like to refuse, for you are known as the local magic man around town. So, if you don't want to disappoint your host or party guests, carry one special playing card in your pocket, just in case they ask you to do a trick. Without this special card, you could not possibly perform this next miraculous piece of magic. Here's a great talking point among your audiences – large and small (that's little tiny people, like me, and giants!).

Since I have told you about the special card, let me tell you what your audience will see should you perform the trick correctly.

A borrowed pack of cards is spread upon the table. One at a time, and very carefully, the performer arranges single cards on to the palm of his hand. When all the cards have been arranged in a circular fashion, the hand is reversed and the entire pack of cards – all fifty two of them – adhere and levitate! The magic man dramatically blows on the cards so they suddenly drop on to the table. Yes – the borrowed pack can be handed out for examination, for it remains as it first was – that of a pack which was loaned to you by the party host.

When it is a rainy day and you don't feel like going out, make up the special card which I was telling you about previously. It consists of two playing cards which have been taken from an old unused pack, perhaps one which has cards already missing. Try to use the ace of spades as one of those, for this particular card usually depicts a rather big ace in the centre of the card. With a model knife or razor blade, cut around part of the ace, one side only, as shown in the illustration. Fold the ace pip upwards so that it forms a hinged portion.

Stick the back of this card on to the second card, using paste or gum. Make sure you don't apply paste to the portion which hinges upwards, for this must be left clean. When pressed down, it should not stick to the card underneath.

Let's explain just how this special card aids the magic man and how it makes possible the levitation of the entire pack to the palm of your hand.

ace pip

pivots upwards

side view

Have this special card hidden inside your pocket and when the time arrives, and you are asked to perform a trick, ask the host for a pack of cards. Emphasize to everyone that these are borrowed cards, which in effect makes the experiment much more convincing and bewildering.

As you turn away to look through the pack, secretly remove the special card from your pocket and add it to the top of the borrowed pack. It does not matter what designed back it has, for this is never shown.

Now that the pack is set, fan the cards and display them freely.

Remove the ace card (special one) from the face of the pack and place it face down on the palm of your hand. In fact, you really make sure that the hinged portion flaps down and protrudes so that this engages between the middle fingers. It can be gripped in this position. This means that should you reverse your hand, the ace would not fall to the floor – but don't please do that at this moment, for there is more to follow.

Begin to pick up individual cards and arrange them *beneath* this special card (between the card and your hand). As you work in a clockwise fashion, you will find it easy to arrange the entire pack of cards, so that all are tightly wedged, either beneath or between other cards. The special card only acts as the one which keeps all secured.

When you reverse your hand you will find that all the cards appear to cling to the back of your hand. If one or two cards fall away, all the better, and please don't apologize, for it still looks very clever, completely convincing and somewhat unexplainable.

When you want the cards to suddenly drop on to the table, blow – or indeed, get a spectator to blow for you. (Blow, I said – *not* SPIT!) But please be quick when displaying the cards at the end, and in passing out the cards for another thorough examination, do make sure you secretly pocket the special card, otherwise you may have yet another talking point to explain later.

31   *The Amazing Cigar Box*

If Dad smokes those small whiff cigars, he will surely
have some empty boxes around the house. If he usually
throws them out, which he should do, really, ask him
nicely to keep you one, for it is this type of box you
need for the following trick. With a little preparation
this box will be capable of doing lots of things for
you. In this specific instance the magic man not only
predicts the chosen cards before they are selected, but
makes his prediction mysteriously appear in ghostly
writing on the inner lid of the box.

You will need a cardboard whiff cigar box, the
type which has a hinged lid.

From a piece of cardboard, cut an additional flap,
an insert which not only fits into the upper lid, but
when it falls, falls nicely into place. On the upper
lid compartment, write, in ghostly fashion (spooky
writing, shaky words), 'three of diamonds ... two of
spades ... seven of clubs' – on the inside lid where
the flap fits.

Beforehand, place the three mentioned cards
against the lid, and on top place the additional flap.
At this stage of the procedure please keep both parts
of the box open. When the box is picked up and
shown, with the flap held tightly against the lid, it
appears to be empty. It is only when the box is actually closed that the inside flap drops and when then
opened, reveals not only the three playing cards, but
the ghostly writing as well.

Paul is no fool – he has used a very old and clever

separate flap

magical principle to bring about this rather updated effect. In the past, only specially made wooden card boxes have been available for magic men to use and perform with. Now the same effect can be performed with this common whiff cigar box, which ultimately looks more natural anyway.

First start showing the box which appears empty. Keep it open at this stage.

From a pack of fifty-two cards, one must be selected

by a spectator. In fact another two spectators should select cards from the pack, resulting in three selected cards. Got it? Stress that all spectators should not look at the cards at this stage and request them to place them, face downwards, into the cigar box. No one ... not even anyone ... not even me ... no one knows the actual values or suits, or both, at this particular moment.

Recap for a few seconds. It helps to break the monotony of it all. Tell your audience that three cards have been freely chosen by various members of your audience, and that these were simply dropped into the cigar box.

The time has come – open the box and point to the three cards inside. Point to the ghostly writing on the upper lid – it does look spooky and it does somehow hint the names of the three cards.

Allow each spectator, in turn, to reverse their cards and let them peer at the ghostly writing on the lid. Yes – all are there – predicted and named correctly. There must be ghosts in the house!

32 Paul's Balmy Bet

Actors and entertainers are a funny lot of people. The other day I bumped into an actor fellow who has been a friend of mine for more years than I should like to remember. He said:

'I've just finished *Breakfast in Bed.*'

I said, 'Did you have a big role?'

'No,' he said, 'just toast and marmalade!'

Which brings me to the point of the real story when in fact we did have lunch together and I challenged him to accept one of my bets. He did, willingly, but lost his money and his pride into the bargain!

From my pocket I removed a packet of plain business cards, secured in the centre by a rather wide elastic band. I also produced a pack of playing cards. I bet my friend that I could predict the name of a playing card which he was later going to cut, within the pack.

He didn't particularly believe me at this stage of the proceedings so he bet one penny (small bets are better than none at all!).

I fanned the pack, closed it up and covered it with my pocket handkerchief. I allowed him to cut the pack through the material of the handkerchief so that we would all be in the dark.

When he lifted the top portion of the pack away, he could finally see his card, the one he cut to, when the handkerchief was removed, of course! I turned my head away at that moment so as not to look at it.

I asked him what his card was, and he told me it was the three of spades.

We put the pack to one side, whilst I started writing the name of a playing card on to the top card of the stack of business cards. He could clearly see me writing 'seven of clubs' on to the card and when I asked him to initial the top portion of the card just to make sure I had not been cheating (I don't cheat –

not a lot – just sometimes!) he realized that I was on a losing stroke, for his cut-at card was definitely not the seven of clubs! His signed card was removed from the packet of plain cards and placed down on to the table before us.

'I'll bet you anything at all that I have written the name of your selected card on to your initialled slip. Take it or leave it,' I told him, 'it's up to you to decide!'

He accepted the chance of winning that penny, but he lost in the end, for when his initialled card was finally reversed, it in fact displayed the three of spades! I shook my head, presented him with the initialled card, as a souvenir, and pocketed my well-earnt penny.

Here's how I did it!

I used a 'force' to make it possible for the spectator to select the three of spades. It's a clever cheeky force that many magic men have used over the years. I'll let you into its secret later.

I also used a batch of plain cards, an elastic band (wide variety) and a *half*-card.

On to one of the cards I scribbled the three of spades (lower portion) and kept the upper space blank. I put this card on top of the others and secured them together with the wide elastic band. The half-card is slid under the elastic band hiding the written card name and so the *top* card appears to be like the others – blank.

When you make your prediction and write the name of the *wrong* card on to this portion, you let the spectator either sign his name or initial the upper section of the top card. Of course, we know he

half card

method of
holding the pack

is really signing the card which will ultimately display the correct card – the three of spades. Fingers
of the right hand grip the top edges of the signed card
and pull it away from the others – but only while the

packet of cards is being reversed. The telltale half-card displaying the 'wrong' card name is taken away with the packet and discarded.

So the spectator bets his money that you are wrong – for he first saw the wrong card name on his signed card. When it is finally reversed, watch his face turn red, for although still signed by himself, the card suddenly displays the name of the chosen card. He's lost his money and his pride!

As for the force of the card, make sure the card on the bottom is the three of spades. Reverse it and another card as well so that two cards remain reversed on the bottom portion of the pack.

Display the pack by removing portions of cards from the top, fanning these, proving they are all different. Cover the pack with your pocket handker-chief. Your right hand holds the pack under the hand-kerchief. Ask a spectator to cut the pack anywhere, but not to remove the top portion, under the hand-kerchief, completely.

When he has made the cut, you secretly reverse the bottom portion so that the two reversed cards are now on top. This means that when the spectator finally removes the upper portion of the pack, from under the handkerchief, the portion left in your right hand appears to show the card which has been cut at. When the 'top' card is removed, that second reversed card still gives the illusion that all the cards are the same way up. If you had to remove that second card, you would give the game away – but ... magic people, you would never do that – would you?

33 *Miraculous Matches*

For years magic men have been shaking boxes of matches and asking innocent spectators, 'Which is the box that is full?' The spectators never win, of course, and the magic man makes sure of that!

Here, I have turned a simple magical effect, one which has been rather over-exposed, into something which can be called different, if not new, in adaptation. If you have any other older magic books at home, you will know what I mean. If the trick is brand new to you, all the better, for I think you are now learning a much better way of presentation. We use three matchboxes, one which is shown to be filled with matches.

The magic man shuffles the boxes around so no one really knows the position of the one which is filled. 'Which matchbox is the full one?' he asks. A spectator points to one, but he is always proved wrong ... and wrong again – always wrong, in fact, silly fellow, for he just cannot possibly win. If only he knew the secret – but he doesn't! In the end the magic man finally shows the spectators the box that really contains the matches. He opens the box, letting them see the matches inside, and suddenly inverts the tray so that the matches should automatically fall to the floor. But they don't – they remain suspended inside – yet another mystery which has to be solved. A magic tap on the tray and the matches are seen to fall on to the floor or table. It's matchic – I mean, magic!

For this trick you require *four* matchboxes, all containing matches.

Secretly hide one of the boxes up your right jacket sleeve using a wide elastic band to retain them there.

Prepare the remaining three matchboxes by snapping a piece from three matchsticks. Each must be shortened enough to wedge across the loose matches inside the boxes. When any of the three inner trays are inverted, the matches stay inside. A simple tap

matchbox
secretly
hidden in sleeve

broken match
holds others
in place

on the back of one of the trays releases the matches so they fall on to the floor.

Have all three matchboxes displayed in a line, on top of your table.

Start the show.

The left hand lifts up the left box and shakes it – it doesn't rattle – it appears to be empty.

The left hand picks up the right-hand box and shakes it also with similar results. The *right* hand picks up the box in the middle and shakes it and it appears to rattle (thanks to the hidden matchbox in the sleeve – that's where the noise comes from). But you can open the box halfway, showing that there are matches inside. Be careful not to reveal the fact that the matches are really wedged inside at this stage of the proceedings.

The three matchboxes are shuffled around and a spectator is requested to point to one, the one which contains the matches.

No matter which box he points to, he can be proved wrong, for the selected box is always shaken with the left hand. It sounds empty. So too, is another box. And the one you wish to be the filled one, is shaken in the right hand, and opened halfway, showing the matches inside.

The trick is repeated several times.

Now for the super suspension illusion! Open the matchbox which appears to contain the matches, turn it upside down, and remove the outer cover. Hokus Pokus – the matches stay inside – suspended. Tap the back of the tray and squeeze the edges, for the matches to fall to the floor. The broken wedged matchstick will fall amongst the others, and the matches can be finally gathered together and placed inside the box.

For the magic man who wants the trick to have a rather surprising climax – this is what to do.

After the 'find the filled matchbox' presentation say: 'I know you are all wondering just how this trick is done – and I'm going to break a rule and tell you – but please keep it a secret!' Open all the matchboxes halfway, revealing that they all contain matches! Tip the matches out on to the table by squeezing the sides of the boxes and take your applause!

34 Putting on a Complete Magic Show

Curtains up, as they say, and if you don't happen to be appearing anywhere where there are curtains – you're on just the same! The show is starting!

It's not that frightening, is it? You have practised all the tricks you intend performing, got everything arranged, and have learnt the patter lines, and all that! But things can still go wrong, believe me.

One theatre I performed in had curtains but it wasn't 'curtains up' as they say in the business. It was curtains DOWN on that night, for a great big blob of curtain material fell on my head as I was just entering. I couldn't really blame the stage manager though, he's my best friend.

The first thing you must do is to plan your act. In preparing his show, the magic man must select the right tricks, blend them together so a nice routine is formed. Your starter must be a trick which is quick and visual and registers well. Your closing item must be sensational so that your audience sends you off with thunderous applause! Between, there should be some good solid magic, tricks which are both baffling and entertaining. There should never be time-wasters. Wasting people's time is simply wasting your own. We don't want the public going home saying, 'Can't remember a single thing he did!' This would mean that none of your tricks really registered or were good enough for your show.

So – my magic people – we want all your friends to go home in a happy mood, asking for more. Keep your show short and to the point. Don't try to give your audience too much at one time. But if you are asked to do more, be careful and resist the wonderful temptation, for you may fall into the magical trap. Audiences hate being bored and magic men who go on and on more than often bore them continuously.

Study the tips and advice given earlier, the ones about appearance, practice and keeping the secrets. These all play a major part in planning a show.

You may need assistants. Your sister, brother or a friend may be able to help you, but like you, they too must keep the secrets! If they don't wish to participate, don't force them. Just place a revolver to their heads and demand that they help you!

Seriously, your assistants can be chosen from your audience. Almost everyone loves to help and assist the magic man. Choose them wisely. You obviously should know the guests at your party and therefore can select those who have a pleasing personality and who are willing to be part of the show. At bigger concerts and fêtes, such as your local school shows, the magic man obviously doesn't know his audience really well. He is faced by strangers who are expecting an entertaining show from him. But if you come over as being a very likeable sort of fellow (or gal), you will get on well. If you demand this, that and the other, treating your audience like prisoners, you will alas not get very far. They may even lift you up and throw you out of the door. Make sure they open it first or you may have a few splinters!

Setting the Show

You will need your magic table. Have the items you require neatly set on top so that you know where each trick is and that it is ready to pick up at a moment's notice.

If you are not quite sure of the running sequence of your tricks, have a slip of paper listing these from start to finish and place it on the table. Remember – it can be disastrous for you should you suddenly pick up your finishing trick somewhere in the middle of your act. Please do try to have some sort of arrangement and running sequence. The simpler the better.

Use Mum's standard lamp near by should you need extra lighting in the home. These's nothing quite like a spot of light entertainment these days!

If you should be presenting your show at a school

concert, on stage, upon a platform, remember you must project your voice so that your audience can hear you loud and clear. The beginner is not advised to use a microphone, even though one might be there, for the purpose of projecting the voice, for such a piece of equipment takes time and practice to master.

Some magic men use their girl assistants for bringing on and taking off (no – not their clothes, silly!) items they require and want to dispose of. If your sister or girlfriend or other willing friend likes the idea of becoming a show-business personality, get her to assist you. Ask her to wear a pretty dress and cue her to come on and go off when you want her to. You must practise all this. It would be rather silly if your assistant came on far too early or too late, and nothing could be worse than watching this happen. The audience must always feel that you know what you are doing and have control over the tricks and assistants in the show.

A large cardboard box, covered in a fancy wallpaper or wrapping paper, is ideal should you require a receptacle to hold all your finished tricks.

Tricks not requiring patter lines can be presented to a suitable musical background. Use your record player or switch your radio on to a suitable programme and let someone operate this, so that when a trick ends he slowly fades the music out. If, on the other hand, you are clever enough to recite patter lines and comedy material, do so, for you will find audiences love this type of presentation. You've got to have the gift of the gab, as they say in the trade! The magic man must be able to chat easily and confidentially, so as to get involved with his audience. I have found no trouble at all – I just open my mouth and the words come out – I wonder who's working me? You've got to be quick-thinking – be a master of ad-libbing (that's answering or telling funny jokes on the spur of the moment) if you want to be a funny man.

To really succeed, you have got to be likeable. Try to make it that way, for if you are putting on a full one-man show, no matter how long, remember, you are the sole attraction. Keep the audience's attention at all times!

And now, here are some suggested acts, using the tricks described in this book. I have listed these so that each blends perfectly and the entire show in each case is extremely well balanced. Good showing – and good luck – magic people!

35 *Suggested Shows . . .*

(using the tricks from my book)

Magic people – if you have learnt ALL of the tricks in this book, and can perform them really well, you can be called a Magic Man. It's nice to be able to perform a trick or two at the drop of the hat, but far better if you can plan your own programmes so that a little group of tricks become a blended routine. In our business we call that an 'act' and several performers have several acts up their sleeves, so that if they appear at the same venues again they will be able to offer their audiences something different on each occasion.

Basically, there are four types of shows for my readers to work on and all use material taken from this book.

But please remember to study the section describing magician's tables, for the magic man will require one during his performance for at least two of the suggested shows which I am about to outline.

Close-Up Show

The tricks used in this impromptu type of show can be performed on any type of table, on top of a chair, or even on the floor itself, if your audience doesn't mind joining you there!

Card-Trick Show

This is quite similar to the close-up show in as much as the card tricks in this book can be presented close up and surrounded.

The wonderful thing about the card-trick show is that, provided the secrets and routines are well planned in one's mind, a borrowed pack of cards is all that is required, and your audience will surely give you credit for being extremely clever. Only a few of the described card tricks actually require specially faked cards, and in more than one instance a 'gimmicked' card can easily be added to a borrowed pack.

Mental Magic Show

Before even considering such a presentation as this, make sure that your patter and appearance match and are both suitable, otherwise this somewhat serious brand of magic may become a farce. Such a presentation is only suitable for entertaining older children and adults. A great number of the 'experiments' (we never call them tricks – although that is what they are) can be performed close up and surrounded.

Platform or Drawing-room Show

Here is the show which will probably make you feel more of a magic man than any other, for you are 'on stage' as we call it, presenting your tricks before a larger audience and using a blended sequence on platform or stage at (perhaps) your local church or organization's annual concert or party. A similar type of show can also be presented at home. Do make sure that your audience is well away from your table and apparatus, and it is best that they remain seated throughout the show. Some of the described close-up tricks can also be used during the platform show, provided these are visual and easy to follow by much larger crowds.

It is wiser to plan several smaller shows rather than one lengthy presentation at first. Shows lasting approximately fifteen minutes are ideal in my opinion – certainly for the beginner to work on and put into practice. Later, when more experienced, through better handling of the tricks themselves and the audiences too, the beginner, now a magic man in his own right, can plan a complete one-hour show of magic, should he want to. Oh – and talking of time – do time your tricks if you want to be perfect so that you will ultimately know just how long the complete act takes to perform. *This is very important.*

Let's start with the
Card-Trick Show. Using a borrowed pack of cards. Begin with:
> *Daylight Robbery* (breezy effect to start with)
> *Here We Are Together*
> *Three in a Row*
> *All Fours* (not a trick but a cute puzzler)
> then for afters – the stunning closer called:
> *The Magic Circle Card Trick*
> Now, here's yet another suggested card-trick show, this time using your own prepared pack of cards.

Start with:
Separating the Reds from the Blacks
Here We Are Together
Find the Lady
and finish with the very strong card levitation:
Magnetic Cards (adding the faked card to the pack).

Of course there are many other card tricks in the book to consider and it is for the individual to select the ones to his liking. Rearrange them if you feel that the sequence flows better for you, but do be careful when planning your opening and closing effects. All four, mentioned above, covering two complete shows, are strong ones and other tricks of a simpler and less effective nature should not follow the closers.

Close-Up Show
 A Hair-Raising Trick
 Fly Away Peter – Fly Away Paul
 Puzzling Polo Mints
 Tricky Trap
 Not a Lot – But What a Knot! and then use the same piece of cord for:
 Cut and Restored Pyjama Cord ... using ...
 Snip! – the cute scissors snipping stunt throughout.

Mental Magic Show
Start with:
 Magic Dice And Dominoes
 Black and Red Mystery
 Paul's Balmy Bet

Three in a Row (taken from our card-trick show) and finish with ...
Any Page ... Any Word ... Anywhere

Platform or Drawing-room Show
Enter:
Commence with one of the several magic wand tricks as described in *Wanderful Magic*.
Magnetic Wand (unfaked version)
or
The Up and Up Wand
A Printer's Dream Come True
Blow Football – The Magic Way
The Perfect Date
The Amazing Cigar Box

Or yet another platform/drawing-room show –
Smartie Wand
The Perfect Date
Knotty Coin Trick
Ten Pence in Every Bun
Puzzling Polo Mints (suitable for both close-up and platform work)

And don't forget Paul's Comedy 'Get-outs' when something horrible goes wrong, like when the trick doesn't work in the end or your table accidentally falls over ... or when you forget what to say or do. I use them all the time and like them a lot – not a lot ... but often on the trot! In fact one television viewer told me confidentially that he enjoyed my get-outs more than my act – was he pulling my leg ... OUCH!

Index

Look out for these terrific Paul Daniels Magic Products

in your shops

1 PAUL DANIELS MAGIC WALLET

One of the most exciting and impressive magic products ever offered to the public. Paul's 10 brilliant card tricks in a smart, mysterious black wallet. Each trick in its own labelled compartment, complete with profusely illustrated booklet. All 10 Paul Daniels Card Tricks also on sale in individual wallets.

2 PAUL DANIELS 20 MAGIC TRICKS

All 20 tricks have been performed by top magicians — many on T.V. You can: make objects disappear from your hand. . . predict numbers. . . 'see' a dice number inside a sealed box! . . . push a pencil through solid glass. . . or miniature swords through a 50p coin . . . make a ball escape from a sealed and tied box while your audience watches the ball! An incredible Magic Box makes cards appear, disappear — even change size! — *lots more*.

3 PAUL DANIELS MAGIC CARDS

A perfectly 'ordinary' pack of cards — yet you can perform 25 remarkable tricks — many performed by top magicians. You can pull individual cards out of the pack. . . find aces. . . 'read' your volunteer's mind and lots more. Fully illustrated instructions.

4 PAUL DANIELS SVENGALI CARDS

12 terrific tricks — plus how to 'palm' and do sleight-of-hand. You can actually predict which cards volunteers will choose. . . or a knife point will touch as the cards fall! . . . actually predict a card *before* a volunteer freely chooses it. Dazzling magic at its best.

5 PAUL DANIELS MARKED DECK CARDS

You can read the back of each card *instantly!* Write up to four card predictions — *before* they're chosen! Display amazing feats of memory. . . read volunteer's minds — even when they're outside the room.

6 *PAUL DANIELS MYSTERY BOX

The most remarkable complete magic act ever offered the public. The box looks empty — yet you can take all kinds of things out of it! Put one thing in. . . make it disappear, reappear. . . or even *change completely!*

Eight fabulous tricks: •Disappearing Coin Rings • Magic Egg •Spot The Ball • All Seeing Eye •Swords Through Coin • Amazing Escape Ball • Genie In The Bottle • Incredible Magic Drawer. Fully illustrated instructions.

7 *PAUL DANIELS MAGIC SPECTACULAR!

A complete Magic Act Paul will show you how to perform really well — plus advanced techniques like palming and sleight of hand. Includes no less than 10 of Paul's favourite tricks — all performed by top magicians — many on T.V.
•Mind Reader Dice • Spot The Ball • Sword Through Coin • Genie In The Bottle • Magic Vanishing Box • Houdini Rings • All Seeing Eye • Coin Through Glass • Magic Cards • TV Magic Card Trick. *Plus:* Magic Wand and Booklet, *Paul Daniels 50 Magic Tricks*. *6 Tricks Magic Box also available.*

*Available early 1981

Paul Daniels T.V. Magic, Dubreq Limited, 120-132 Cricklewood Lane, London NW2 2DP.